Grade 2
Jumbo Workbook

This workbook belongs to:

Use pencils, crayons, and stickers to complete the activities in this book. When there is a sticker missing, you will see this pattern:

Dear Parents,

Welcome to the *Grade 2 Jumbo Workbook!*

Here are some tips to help ensure that your child gets the most from this book.

★ Look at the pages with your child, ensuring he or she knows what to do before starting.

★ Plan short, regular sessions, only doing one or two pages at a time.

★ Praise your child's efforts and improvements.

★ Encourage your child to assess his or her own efforts in a positive way. For example, say: "You've written some great C's there. Which one do you think you did best?"

★ Make the learning sessions positive experiences. Give prompts where they might help. If a section is too hard for your child, leave those pages until he or she is ready for them.

★ Relate the learning to things in your child's world. For example, if your child is working on a page about plants, ask him or her to identify some plants in your home or community.

★ There are stickers to use throughout the book. They help build your child's hand-eye coordination and observation skills. Encourage your child to place the stickers on each page before starting the other activities. There are also reward stickers to help increase motivation.

★ At the back of the workbook is an answer section. Encourage your child to attempt the activities and check them over before looking at the answers. Some activities have open questions with no right or wrong answer. Help your child to recognize these activities and to use self-expression.

Together, the activities in the workbook help build a solid understanding of core learning concepts and topics to ensure your child is ready for third grade.

We wish your child hours of enjoyment with this fun workbook!

Scholastic Early Learning

Picture credits: All photos courtesy of **Shutterstock,** unless noted as follows:
aleks333/Shutterstock.com: 28ml (girls sitting); **Darq/Shutterstock.com:** 142tm (red car);
MBI Images: 7br (dinosaur), 50bl (pirate boy), 50br (princess), 67cl (drum), 75bl (boy
throwing), 83tr (dinosaur), 104blm (black hair doll), 104blm (red hair doll), 181tm (strawberry),
181m (sandwich), 184mr (green ruler), 186br (block being juggled), 224tr (dog), 224tr
(parrot), 224mr (lizard), 224br (fish), 225tr (bear), 229bl (cupcake), Sticker sheet 5tr (rabbits),
Sticker sheet 6mr (flower), Sticker sheet 9tl (orange sweet); **Michael Shake/Shutterstock.com:**
142t, Sticker sheet 8tl (silver car); **phortun/Shutterstock.com:** 33mr (Frida Kahlo).

Contents

Anna

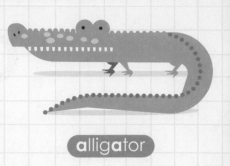

alligator

Trace and write **a**'s. Then circle the neatest one in each row.

A A

a a

Write this sentence.

An anteater can eat 30,000 ants in a day.

Write these words in alphabetical order.

alphabet again **away** America **ahead** astronaut

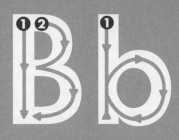

Bobby

baseball

Trace and write **b**'s. Then circle the neatest one in each row.

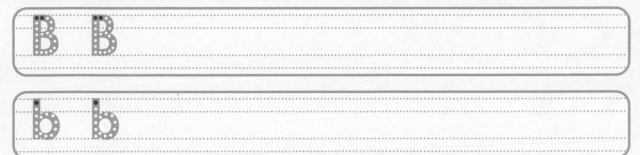

Write this sentence.

Warm basketballs have the best bounce.

Write these words in alphabetical order.

bubble   blueberry   Brazil   baboon   blubber   baby

Caleb

comic

Trace and write **c**'s. Then circle the neatest one in each row.

C C

c c

Write this sentence.

A collection of crabs is called a cast.

Write these words in alphabetical order.

click cocoon **circus** China **catch** cactus

Daisy

daffodil

Trace and write **d**'s. Then circle the neatest one in each row.

D D

d d

Write this sentence.

Diplodocus was a dinosaur that didn't eat meat.

Write these words in alphabetical order.

drive   dodge   December   did   dance   dish

Trace and write **e**'s. Circle the neatest one.

E E

e e

Write this sentence.

Energetic exercise helps us feel better.

Trace and write **f**'s. Circle the neatest one.

F F

f f

Write this sentence.

Arctic foxes have fluffy fur on their feet.

George

giggle

Trace and write **g**'s. Then circle the neatest one in each row.

G G

g g

Write this sentence.

Great Dane dogs can grow bigger than people.

Write these words in alphabetical order.

garbage   goggles   gaming   garage   Greenland

Hannah

headphones

Trace and write **h**'s. Then circle the neatest one in each row.

H H

h h

Write this sentence.

Laughing helps the heart stay healthy.

Write these words in alphabetical order.

horse high **Hawaii** hour **hippo** hundred

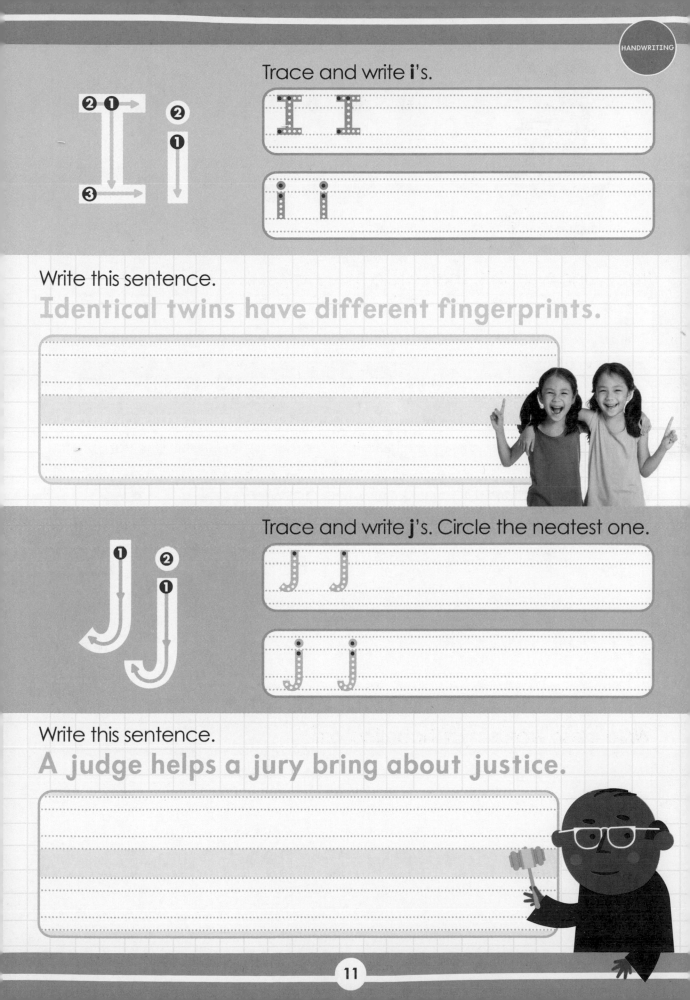

Trace and write **i**'s.

I I

i i

Write this sentence.

Identical twins have different fingerprints.

Trace and write **j**'s. Circle the neatest one.

J J

j j

Write this sentence.

A judge helps a jury bring about justice.

Kenny

kick

Trace and write **k**'s. Then circle the neatest one in each row.

K K

k k

Write this question. Do you know the answer?
Where do kangaroos and koalas live?

Write these words in alphabetical order.

knight Kansas **knee** kind **know** kitchen

Lucy

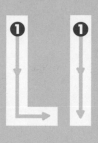

llama

Trace and write **l**'s. Then circle the neatest one in each row.

L L

l l

Write this sentence.

Leopards like to lie on long branches.

Write these words in alphabetical order.

level   lizard   London   likely   long   loyal

Matt

M m

mammoth

Trace and write **m**'s. Then circle the neatest one in each row.

M M M

m m

Write this sentence.

The Moon has many mild moonquakes.

Write these words in alphabetical order.

Monday mammal **mermaid** mix **mime** mouth

Nina

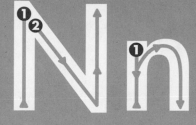

noon

Trace and write **n**'s. Then circle the neatest one in each row.

N N

n n

Write this sentence.

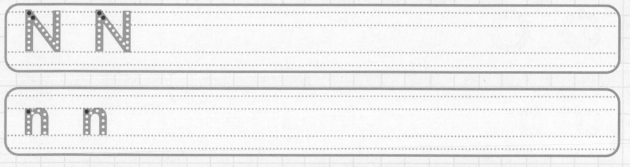

Nonsense poems make no sense.

Write these words in alphabetical order.

none ninja **noise** November **never** next

Oliver

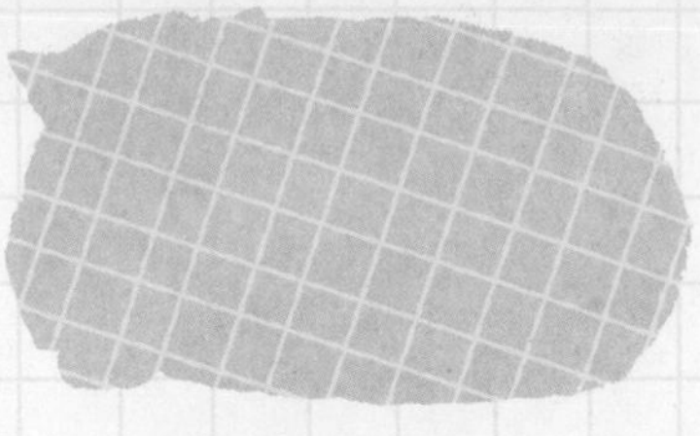

ocelot

Trace and write o's. Then circle the neatest one in each row.

Write this sentence.

Octopuses have no nose and no skeleton.

Write these words in alphabetical order.

October   oil   our   order   okay   odd

Trace and write **p**'s.

P P

p p

Write this sentence.

Porcupine prickles are not poisonous.

Trace and write **q**'s. Circle the neatest one.

Q Q

q q

Write this sentence.

Keep quiet during a quick quiz.

R r

Ruby

recorder

Trace and write **r**'s. Then circle the neatest one in each row.

R R

r r

Write this sentence.

The white rhinoceros is really rare.

Write these words in alphabetical order.

referee ruler **race** Russia **rain** relax

Sam

S s

sisters

Trace and write **s**'s. Then circle the neatest one in each row.

S s

s s

Write this sentence.

The sluggish sloth sleeps in trees.

Write these words in alphabetical order.

Sunday **star** **shoes** **season** **scissors** **stink**

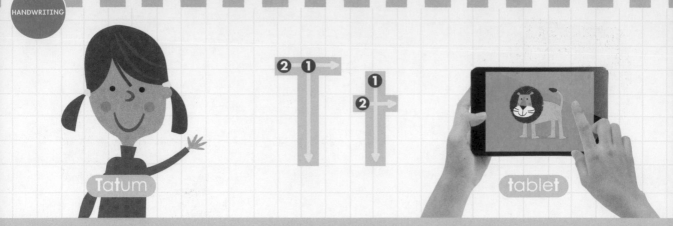

Tatum

tablet

Trace and write **t**'s. Then circle the neatest one in each row.

Write this sentence.

Turtles and tortoises have no teeth.

Write these words in alphabetical order.

tight Tuesday **tent** that **taste** thirsty

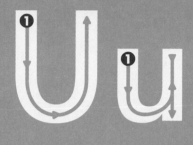

Uri

umbrella

Trace and write **u**'s. Then circle the neatest one in each row.

Write this sentence.

You are unlikely to see a unicorn or a UFO.

Write these words in alphabetical order.

usual **under** ukulele **Utah** use uniform

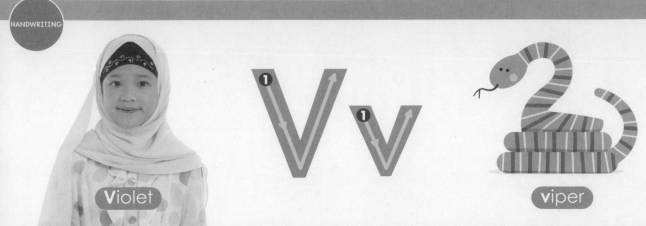

Violet

viper

Trace and write **v**'s. Then circle the neatest one in each row.

V V

v v

Write this sentence.

Vet is short for veterinarian and veteran.

Write these words in alphabetical order.

violin Viking van video vulture vote

Trace and write **w**'s.

W W

w w

Write this sentence.

Worms wiggle up when the weather is wet.

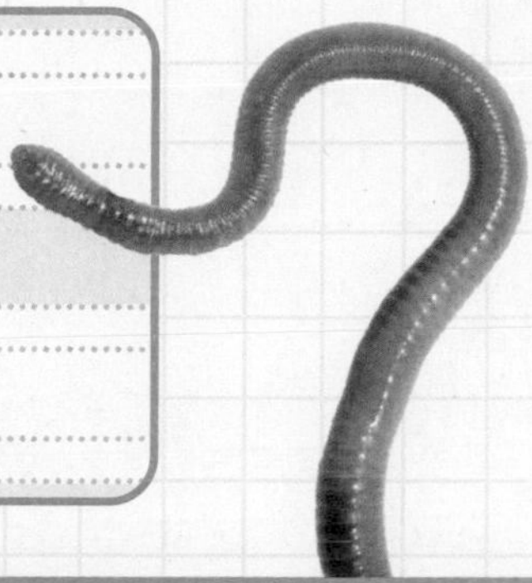

Trace and write **x**'s. Circle the neatest one.

X X

x x

Write these sentences.

X often comes after e. Exam is an example.

Yasmin

yawn

Trace and write **y**'s. Then circle the neatest one in each row.

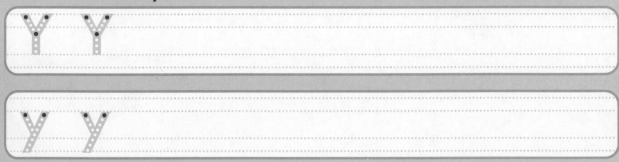

Y Y

y y

Write this sentence.

Yelp, yell, yodel, and yap are all sound words.

Write these words in alphabetical order.

yesterday   Yemen   yellow   yes   year   yo-yo

Zz

Zach

zigzag

Trace and write **z**'s. Then circle the neatest one in each row.

Z Z

z z

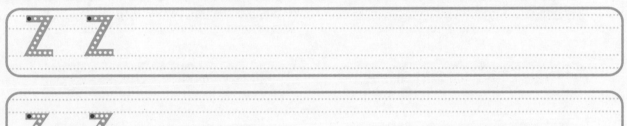

Write this sentence.

Zilch means the same thing as zero.

Write these words in alphabetical order.

zebra   Zanzibar   zone   zoo   zap   zither

Book Titles

Each main word in a title starts with a capital letter.

Circle the title with the correct capital letters in each pair.

(How to Play the Guitar)	**How to play the guitar**
Max's wilderness adventure	**Max's Wilderness Adventure**
Tales of Brave Princesses	**Tales of brave princesses**
Learn the Rules of Football	**Learn The rules of Football**
Rescue at red ridge	**Rescue at Red Ridge**

Write titles for these books. Start the main words with capital letters.

The Main Idea

The **main idea** of a text or paragraph is the topic that covers all of it.

Read the text and then answer the questions below.

Living Reefs

Coral reefs are beautiful underwater worlds, teeming with life. Creatures such as fish, turtles, and squid dart about, filling the water with color.

Even the coral itself is alive. A coral polyp is like a tiny jellyfish living inside a hard shell that is joined to other coral shells. Different coral species have different colors and shapes. Millions of old coral shells join up to form a reef.

Fish of all shapes and sizes live on coral reefs. The smallest fish eat tiny plants and animals called plankton. These small fish are eaten by bigger fish, which are then eaten by even bigger fish. The biggest fish of all are the sharks.

What is the main idea for the whole text? ....

....

What is the main idea of the second paragraph? ....

....

What is the main idea of the third paragraph? ....

....

The Details

> The **details** are the different points that help explain the main idea.

Read the text, looking out for details as you read.

Learning in Ancient Egypt

If you had been a child in Ancient Egypt, your life would have been very different. Most children didn't go to school or learn to read or write.

A few girls trained for special roles, such as being a priestess. Most, however, learned homemaking and farming skills from their family. At about 12 years old, they got married.

Most boys learned skills such as farming, metalwork, or building. Some learned to paint, and a few trained to be scribes. The scribes were the only people who could read and write and so they had high status.

What role would you have liked if you had lived back then?

A young scribe from Ancient Egypt

What is the main idea? ....

....

List three details from the text.

1 ....

2 ....

3 ....

Context Clues

Context clues are clues to a word's meaning found in the nearby text and pictures.

Use the sentence to figure out the meaning of the word in **bold**.
Circle the correct meaning.

1 Logan picked a bunch of sweet-smelling **nasturtiums** and put them in a vase.

    nasty germs   **a type of insect**   **a type of flower**

2 The family found a **secluded** spot, far from the other beach goers.

    busy and noisy   **quiet and private**   **full of seashells**

3 Ethan was a **finicky** eater, and his aunt could find nothing he would eat.

    tidy   **greedy**   **fussy**

4 The movers used a **hoist** to lift the piano up to the second story.

    a special type of hose   **a machine for lifting heavy objects**

5 The ball **ricocheted** off the goalpost, back toward the soccer player.

    bounced off   **fell off**   **climbed off**

6 At last, the seeds **germinated** and we saw their first shoots.

    died   **started to grow**   **turned pink**

Look up each word in a dictionary. Then write a sentence that would help others understand it.

hoarse ....

mandatory ....

Fiction

Fiction texts are not true; they are made-up stories.

Things that cannot happen in real life often happen in fiction books. Circle the books that are most likely to be fiction.

Robbie Rabbit Starts School

Birds of America

Life in Ancient Rome

Milly the Magical Fairy

How to Paint Like a Pro

Superheroes to the Rescue

Design a cover for a fiction book and a nonfiction book, and write the titles.

Fiction

Nonfiction

Fables

A **fable** is a story that teaches us a lesson, or moral.

Long ago, a Greek man known as Aesop wrote many fables. Read this one, and circle the correct answers below.

The Lion and the Mouse

One summer's day, a mouse ran over a lion's nose. The lion woke and swiped up the mouse in his huge paw.

"How dare you wake me," the lion said. "I will swallow you in one gulp."

"Please let me go," said the shaking mouse. "I promise I will repay you."

"Ha!" said the lion. "A mouse could never repay a mighty lion, but I will let you go since you asked nicely."

A few days later, the lion fell into a hunter's trap. He roared for help, but none of the other animals dared come near. Then, at last, a small voice spoke up.

"I'll help you," said the mouse, and she nibbled and gnawed at the ropes until, at last, she set the lion free.

"See," she said, "even a mouse can help a lion."

1 Why didn't the lion think a mouse could help him?

Mice are much smaller than lions.   **Mice are much meaner than lions.**

2 Why did the mouse save the lion?

To stop lions becoming extinct.   **To repay him for letting her go.**

3 Circle the two morals that could go with this story.

Beauty is only skin deep.   **A kind deed is never wasted.**

No one is too small to help others.   **Slow and steady wins the race.**

Folktales

A **folktale** is an old story passed down over many years by word-of-mouth.

Read this folktale from China, and circle the correct answers below.

The New Year Monster

Long, long ago, there was a terrible monster known as Nian. Each New Year, Nian came down from the hills to attack the villagers. One year, an old man visited the village.

"Lock your door tonight or Nian will get you," the people warned him.

"Don't worry," he said. "I will get rid of Nian for you."

That night, the villagers locked their doors and huddled inside. At about midnight, they heard Nian scratching and sniffing around their homes. No one dared move or make a sound.

Suddenly, loud bangs filled the air. Peering outside, the villagers saw red lanterns in the road and bright lights exploding into the sky. They saw Nian fleeing back to the hills. The old man had scared the monster away.

Ever since then, Chinese people have celebrated New Year with red lanterns and fireworks.

1   What is this story meant to explain?
Why people light red lanterns and fireworks at New Year.
Why monsters are scared of old men.

2   Why were most folktales passed down by word-of-mouth?
Because most people talked too much.
Because most people couldn't write.

3   Why might modern Chinese people tell this story to their children?
To warn them about Nian.
To keep alive an old story.

Biographies

A **biography** is a description of a real person's life.

Read this short biography.

Frida Kahlo (1907–1954)

Frida Kahlo was a famous artist, but she had a tough life. She was born in Mexico in 1907. At age 6, she caught a disease called polio and had to stay in bed for nine months. She was left with one leg shorter than the other.

Frida was one of the first girls to attend a famous high school in Mexico. She did well there, but then, when she was 18, she was in a traffic accident and nearly died. Stuck in bed, she filled her days with painting.

An artist called Diego Rivera liked both Frida and her art. In time, they were married and traveled the world. However, Frida always missed Mexico. She wore Mexican dresses and painted many colorful self-portraits.

1 What two things was Frida lucky to survive? ....

....

2 Do you think Frida's accidents could have helped her become an artist? Why? ....

....

3 The years in the title tell us when Frida was born and when she died. Did she have a long life? How can you tell? ....

....

Characters

The **characters** are the people or talking animals in a story.

Read this story that has three main characters.

The Challenge

Ella, Luke, and Henry were in the same math group. Their teacher gave them some puzzle pieces.

"Your goal is to make a square with these pieces," she said.

The children moved the pieces into different shapes, but they couldn't make a square.

"This is stupid," Henry said. "I give up." He stood up and went back to his desk.

"Hmm," said Luke, "there must be a way."

"We could sneak a look at the other groups," Ella said.

"No," said Luke, "that's cheating. Let's try putting these straight sides together."

Ella and Luke kept trying. At last, they figured it out.

"It feels good to have solved it," Ella said. "I'm glad we didn't cheat."

Henry   Ella   Luke

Reread the story, and then write a sentence about each character.

Henry: ....

Ella: ....

Luke: ....

Points of View

A character's **point of view** is his or her thoughts and opinions on a topic.

Read this story and compare Grace and Joe's points of view.

"Happy birthday!" Mom said. "What would you like to do today?"

The twins looked at each other.

"It's really hot. I'd like to go to the pool for a swim," Grace said.

"No, it will be too crowded today," Joe said. "Let's go to a movie. It will be cool inside the theater."

"But I don't want to be in the dark on such a sunny day," Grace replied.

"Well, I don't want to be in the hot, burning sun," Joe said.

"Oh, dear," said Mom. "We'll have to stay home if you can't agree. What would you like for dinner?"

Continue the story, giving Grace and Joe different points of view. Make sure each one has a reason for their choice.

....

....

....

....

....

....

An Opinion Piece

In an **opinion** text, a writer tells us their own thoughts and ideas.

Read this opinion text.

My Terrible Neighbors

I think the family next door should move away. They are terrible!

Every afternoon, the children go into their yard. They throw balls, ride bikes, and jump on their trampoline. They make lots of noise, always laughing and shouting.

Their dog runs around, too. It chases balls and barks when it is excited.

Worst of all, the little ones play the recorder. I can hear their loud squawks as they play songs together.

If this family moved out, a quiet one might move in. My life would be so much better.

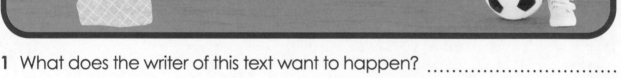

1 What does the writer of this text want to happen? ....

....

2 Underline each of the writer's reasons in different colors.

3 Do you agree with this person's opinion? Why or why not? ....

....

4 What sort of person do you think might write something like this? ....

....

A Different Version

Sometimes writers take an old story and write a new, **different version.**

Read this story. What story does it remind you of?

The Three Pirates

Long ago, three pirates were shipwrecked on a deserted island. Each pirate built himself a home.

The first pirate cut grass and made a grass hut. It took a week to make. The second pirate picked up sticks and built a wooden hut. It took a month to make. The third pirate made bricks from clay and built a brick house. It took a year to make.

One day, a terrible storm hit the island. First, it blew down the grass hut. The pirate rushed to the wooden hut for shelter. Soon, however, the wooden hut blew apart. The pirates ran to the brick house.

The brick house was strong and survived the winds. After the storm, the first and second pirates built brick homes of their own.

1 What fairy tale is this story based on? ....

2 The writer has used pirates instead of .... and has used

a storm instead of the ....

3 How are the two stories similar? ....

....

4 Write a moral, or lesson, for this story. ....

....

Nonsense Poems

Nonsense poems often have made-up words. Sometimes, they don't make sense.

Read this nonsense poem by Laura E. Richards.

Eletelephony

Once there was an elephant,
Who tried to use the telephant—
No! No! I mean an elephone
Who tried to use the telephone—
(Dear me! I am not certain quite
That even now I've got it right.)

Howe'er it was, he got his trunk
Entangled in the telephunk;
The more he tried to get it free,
The louder buzzed the telephee—
(I fear I'd better drop the song
Of elephop and telephong!)

1 What happened to the elephant in this poem?

....

2 Look at the words at the ends of the lines. Underline each pair of rhyming words with a different colored pencil.

3 What real words did the poet use to make these nonsense words?

telephant ....

elephone ....

telephunk ....

4 Make up some nonsense words using parts of these words: television, hippopotamus, computer, rhinoceros.

....

....

Poems About Feelings

Poets often write about their **thoughts and feelings.**

Read this poem by Robert Louis Stevenson.

Bed in Summer

In Winter, I get up at night
And dress by yellow candle light.
In Summer, quite the other way,
I have to go to bed by day.

I have to go to bed and see
The birds still hopping on the tree,
Or hear the grown-up people's feet
Still going past me in the street.

And does it not seem hard to you,
When all the sky is clear and blue,
And I should like so much to play,
To have to go to bed by day?

1 What doesn't the child in this poem like doing? Do you feel the same way?
   Why? ....

   ....

2 Circle the pairs of rhyming words at the ends of the lines.

3 Underline the words **_have to go to bed_** each time they occur in the
   poem. Why do you think the poet repeated these words?

   ....

4 What clue in the first stanza tells you that this poem was written long ago?

   ....

Step-by-Step Instructions

Step-by-step instructions tell us how to do things. They often start with a list of things you need.

Read the step-by-step instructions, fill in the missing words, and draw the missing pictures.

Make a Model Volcano

You will need:

- a tray
- a small jar
- modeling clay
- 2 teaspoons baking soda
- 1 teaspoon dish soap
- 4 drops red food coloring
- ¼ cup vinegar

1

On the tray, make a mountain shape out of the modeling ....

2

Mold the jar into the top of the mountain.

3

Put the baking ...., food ...., and dish .... into the jar.

4

Carefully pour in the vinegar, and then step back!

Note: Ask a parent's permission before trying this activity. It is best done outside.

Story Structure

Stories have a **beginning**, a **middle**, and an **end**.

Read the beginning and middle of this story. Then write an ending.

Beach Rescue

Abby and Noah were staying at their uncle's house by the beach.

"Don't go in the water without me," Uncle James said. "It's too dangerous."

"We won't," they said and headed off to explore some rock pools.

Noah found some shrimp and a starfish in one rock pool. Abby found some little fish and a tiny blue crab in another.

"I wonder what's in the rock pools in the next bay," said Noah.

"Let's go and look," said Abby.

They climbed around the rocks and found some deeper rock pools. One had a purple jellyfish in it.

After a few hours, the children's stomachs began to rumble.

"Let's go back for lunch," Noah said.

"Oh, no!" said Abby, looking up. "The tide has come in. We can't get back!"

....

....

....

....

....

....

Question Words

Texts often answer these questions: who, what, where, why, and how.

Read this newspaper article and answer the questions below.

The Shoe Thief

In suburban Berlin, a thief was stealing people's shoes. If someone left their shoes outside at night, they were gone in the morning.

A man became angry when his new sneakers went missing. He decided to track down the thief, and that's when he got a surprise.

He saw the thief carrying away a pair of blue flip-flops. It was a fox! The man followed the fox back to its den. There he found more than 100 pairs of shoes.

No one knows for sure why the fox took the shoes. Perhaps it liked the smell.

What was the problem? ....

Who was the thief? ....

What did the thief steal? ....

Where did this story take place? ....

How did the man find the shoes? ....

When did the shoes go missing? ....

Why did the fox take the shoes? ....

The Five Senses

Writers often tell us what things look, taste, sound, smell, and feel like.

Read the story, looking out for text about the senses.

Ocean Swim

Anna had never been to an ocean before. She could hear the roaring waves crashing onto the beach. The grainy sand below her feet was pale gray and, in front of her, sparkling blue water stretched out as far as she could see.

Anna dipped her toes into the water and then whipped them out again.

"It's cold!" she told her brother.

Slowly, bit by bit, she edged her way into the water. It felt a little warmer once she was used to it, and she started having fun. Then a wave knocked her over and she swallowed some seawater.

"Yuck, it's salty!" she said. "I'm getting out. Besides, I can smell the smoke from Dad's barbecue now. It's making me hungry."

Describe something Anna **saw.** ....

....

Describe something Anna **heard.** ....

....

Describe something Anna **felt.** ....

....

Describe something Anna **tasted.** ....

....

Describe something Anna **smelled.** ....

....

Similes and Metaphors

A **simile** is a phrase that compares two things using words such as *like* or *as*.
A **metaphor** compares two things by saying that they are the same thing.

Read each sentence, and then check either simile or metaphor.

	Simile	Metaphor
She runs like a racehorse.	✓	
You are a star!		✓
Their room is a pigsty.		
Mia was as quiet as a mouse.		
His brain is a super computer.		
She has the heart of a lion.		
He growled like a bear.		
The storm struck like a wild beast.		
Her hair is a river of gold.		
My bag is as light as a feather.		
My teacher is as busy as a bee.		
His stomach is a bottomless pit.		

Make up a new simile and metaphor.

He is as .... as ....

She is a ....

Inferencing

Inferencing is using the clues in a text to figure out something the writer does not tell you.

Read the text and use the clues to circle the correct answer.

1 Just before her mom came in, Julie turned off the light and shut her eyes.

What did Julie want her mother to think?

That she was awake.   That she was reading.   That she was asleep.

2 Alex shivered as he pulled on his hat and zipped up his jacket.

What sort of day was it?

hot   **cold**   **warm**

3 Mrs. Jones blew her whistle and called the players in from the field.

What subject was Mrs. Jones teaching?

gym   **math**   **art**

4 When David saw his dinner plate, his face fell and his shoulders drooped.

What was David's opinion about his dinner?

It looked okay.   He didn't like it.   It was his favorite.

5 Lizzy dropped the pan and rushed to put her hand in cold water.

What had happened?

Lizzy had finished cooking.   Lizzy had burned her hand.

6 Dan pushed on the pedals as hard as he could to get there faster.

How is Dan traveling?

He is on a bus.   He is in a train.   He is on a bike.

Exciting Starts

Writers often make the **start** of a story exciting to catch the readers' interest.

Read about three ways writers often start their stories. Then read the story starter and answer the questions below.

Secrets to a Good Start

1 Start with a short sentence.

2 Introduce your character and setting.

3 Include a problem that makes readers want to find out what happens next.

"Help!" yelled George. "My boat is sinking."
    He could see people on the shore, but they couldn't hear his shouts. How could he get them to notice him?

1 Is the first sentence long or short?   long   short

2 Who is the main character and where is he?

....

....

3 What does the reader want to find out?

....

....

4 Write what you think might happen next in this story.

....

....

....

....

Good Endings

The **ending** of a story often happens when a problem is solved.

Check the ending that solves the problem for each story idea.

1 Jacob finds a treasure map in an old chest. He wonders what the treasure could be.

   A Jacob puts the map in the trash and forgets about it. ☐

   B Jacob uses the map to find the treasure. ☐

2 Zoey wants to play basketball, but she can't make a basket.

   A Zoey practices until she can make a basket and join a team. ☐

   B Zoey gives up and decides she hates basketball. ☐

Plan an ending that solves the problem in each story idea below.

1 Ella and Eva are twins. No one can tell them apart, and they don't like it.

....

....

....

....

....

2 Josh's rocket has crash landed on a strange planet. How will he get home?

....

....

....

....

....

Linking Words

> Linking words and phrases help us join ideas together.
> They include: because, also, then, but, so, so that, unless, either ... or.

Underline the linking words in each line.

1 I want to go swimming, but it is too cold today.

2 Sophie missed her grandma, so she wrote her a letter.

3 We won't finish in time unless you help us.

4 We had a party because it was Dad's birthday.

5 Harry shut the gate so that the dog wouldn't get out.

6 Bike riding is fun. It also keeps you fit.

7 He ate his pasta. Then he had dessert.

8 Bring either a coat or a jacket.

Write endings to these sentences.

1 Emma is very small, but ....

2 Ben lost his shoes, so ....

3 You will miss the bus unless ....

4 She wore her best dress because ....

5 I feed the birds in winter so that ....

6 Last week, we visited our cousins. We also ....

7 He did his chores. Then ....

8 For lunch, you can have either .... or ....

Character Differences

The characters are the people or animals in a story.
They can have **differences** and **similarities** with one another.

Read Matt's recall story about his family's picnic.

On Saturday, we went to the park for a picnic. It was horrible. The weather was too hot. My brother Sam played ball with some other children. I didn't want to, so I had nothing to do. Dad brought chicken salad for lunch. I don't like chicken salad. I did like the lemonade, though. The best part of the day was going home.

Now pretend you are Matt's brother Sam. Write about the same picnic. Show some ways Sam is different from Matt and one way he is the same.

On Saturday, we went to the park for a picnic. It was great. ....

....

....

....

....

....

....

Create a Character

The best characters seem real. Writers often plan their characters before they write.

Plan a character for a story. It could be a child, an animal, a pirate, a princess, or anyone you want.

Character's name: .... Character's age: ....

What the character looks like: ....

....

Where the character lives: ....

Things the character likes to do: ....

....

Things the character is scared of: ....

....

The character's greatest skill or talent: ....

The character's greatest weakness: ....

What the character wants most of all: ....

....

....

Write a Story

When writing a story, tell your readers about the characters' actions, words, and feelings. Use linking words, and show the solution to a problem at the end.

Put the character you created on page 50 into a story.

The title of the story is: ....

The beginning: ....
....
....
....

The middle: ....
....
....
....
....
....
....

The end: ....
....
....
....

Settings

Writers choose a **place** to **set** each story. They describe that place to their readers.

Choose a place you love to go and write notes about it here:

The place is ....

When you are there, you can see ....

....

You can hear ....

You might smell ....

Write a paragraph about a time you were at this place.
Include information about things you saw, heard, and smelled.

....

....

....

....

....

....

....

....

....

....

....

....

....

....

Write a Poem

Words are made up of units of sound called **syllables**.
We can count syllables like this: sun (1); sun/ny (2); sun/glass/es (3).

A haiku is a Japanese poem of 3 lines. The first and last line have 5 syllables. The middle line has 7 syllables. Read these haikus and count the syllables. Then write a haiku of your own.

Now it is summer,
we love to swim in the pool.
These are the best days.

What is that I see?
A little green grasshopper
is hiding from me.

Some days, we are friends.
Some days, we argue and fight.
We are true brothers.

....

(5 syllables)

....

(7 syllables)

....

(5 syllables)

Reasons for Writing

Writers write different texts depending on their reason, or **purpose**, for writing.

Read the two texts. Then answer the questions below.

Ants are amazing insects. They live in huge groups headed by a queen ant, who lays eggs. The worker ants collect food and care for the babies. They also build the nest, making tunnels, storerooms, and rooms for resting in. Some ants also help hurt ants get back to the nest to recover.

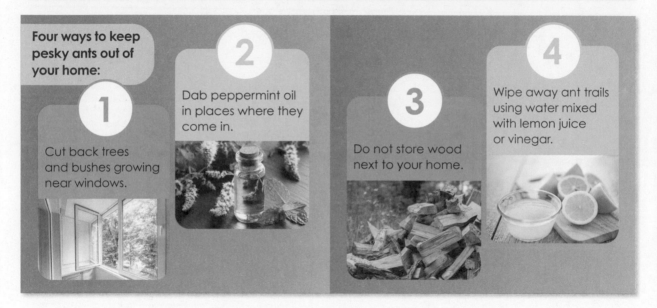

Four ways to keep pesky ants out of your home:

1 Cut back trees and bushes growing near windows.

2 Dab peppermint oil in places where they come in.

3 Do not store wood next to your home.

4 Wipe away ant trails using water mixed with lemon juice or vinegar.

1 In what way are the two texts similar? ....

....

2 In what way are they different? ....

....

3 In what sort of reading material might you find the first text?

....

4 In what sort of reading material might you find the second text?

....

Write About Dragons

Writers write different texts for different types of reading matter.

Imagine that dragons are real, and write two different texts about them.

1 Write a paragraph for a science website telling people about where dragons live and what they do.

....
....
....
....
....
....

2 Write a paragraph for a magazine telling people how to stay safe around dragons.

....
....
....
....
....
....

Retell a Story

To **retell** a story, introduce the characters and what they want.
Tell the reader about the characters' actions and what happens in the end.

Choose a favorite book or movie that you know well.
Retell the story here.

The title of the story is: ....

The beginning: ....

....

....

....

....

The middle: ....

....

....

....

....

....

The end: ....

....

....

Write a Fantasy

Fantasy stories are about things that are not real or are unknown, such as monsters, fairies, or aliens.

Choose one of these fantasy ideas or make up your own. Then write your fantasy story.

1 You are a secret superhero who saves your school from a monster.

2 You find fairies in your backyard, but no one believes you.

3 Some aliens take you to their planet. What happens there?

The title of the story is: ....

The beginning: ....
....
....
....

The middle: ....
....
....
....

The end: ....
....
....

Interview Someone

Non-fiction writers talk to other people, or **interview** them, to learn new things.

Find out what it is like to do a particular job. Interview a parent or other trusted adult about their job. Here are some questions to ask.

1 What job do you do? ....

2 What hours do you work? ....

3 What tasks do you do? ....

....

....

4 What do you like about your job? ....

....

....

5 What is hard about your job? ....

....

....

Ask other questions that interest you, and write notes here.

....

....

....

....

Write About a Job

After interviewing people, non-fiction writers tell others about what they have learned.

Use your interview notes to write about the job you discussed. Include facts about the job as well as the person's thoughts and opinions on it.

What It's Like to Be a ....

My .... is a ....

....

....

....

....

....

....

....

....

I **would like/ would not like** to have this job because ....

....

....

Write a Letter

A **letter** is a formal way of writing a message.

Read Ellie's letter to her friend Hazel. Then write Hazel's reply.

25 Oak Avenue
Springtown
May 5, 2021

Dear Hazel,

Hi, are you enjoying the big city? It is not the same here without you.
I miss your funny jokes and the way you helped me with math.

We have a class pet now. It is a goldfish called Gary.
What is your new school like? Is it bigger than our country school?
Do you have any class pets? Have you made new friends?

Love from,
Ellie James

463 Station Street
Slate City
May 12, 2021

Dear Ellie,

....

....

....

....

....

Love from,
Hazel Green

Address an Envelope

When sending paper letters, write the **address** of the person
you are writing to on the front of the **envelope**.

Here is the envelope from Ellie's letter to Hazel. Add the stamp.
Then underline Hazel's name in **red** and her address in **blue**.

Hazel Green

463 Station Street

Slate City

Address this envelope to yourself or someone you know.

....

....

....

....

Write Instructions

Step-by-step instructions often start with a list of things you need.
After this comes the numbered steps.

Think of something you know how to do. It could be riding a bike, brushing your teeth, or making an ice-cream sundae.
Write instructions that tell someone else how to do it.

How to ....

You will need:

- ....

- ....

- ....

- ....

What to do:

1 ....

....

2 ....

....

3 ....

....

4 ....

....

5 ....

....

6 ....

Research and Plan

A **non-fiction** text tells readers about something real or true.

Choose a non-fiction topic you would like to know more about. It could be a place, a type of animal, or a topic from history or science.

My topic idea is ....

Use the Internet, library books, or encyclopedias to research your topic. Jot down short notes about things you find interesting here.

....

....

....

....

....

....

....

....

....

Decide which part of the topic you would like to write an article about.

I'd like to write about ....

Draft an Article

For important pieces of text, writers often make a **rough draft** first.

Write the first draft of your article. Introduce the topic, and then add some interesting facts. Sum it up with a closing sentence.

....
....
....
....
....
....
....
....
....
....
....
....
....
....
....

Read your draft aloud. Then make these checks:

1 Circle any spellings you need to check in a dictionary.

2 Check your sentences start with a capital letter and end with a period.

3 Make sure your sentences make sense.

4 Decide which parts you want to change or improve.

Write an Article

Writers write a **final version** of a text using their draft and making changes to improve it.

Write the final version of your article here. Include a title.

....

....

....

....

....

....

....

....

....

....

....

....

....

....

....

....

....

....

....

Draw a picture to go with it.

Count Syllables

Words are made up of sounds called **syllables**.
We break words into syllables like this: dog, pup/py, di/no/saur.

Say and clap each syllable.	Write the word with a slash between each syllable.	How many syllables does it have?
panda	pan/da	2
winter		
umbrella		
caterpillar		
crayon		
alphabet		

Draw lines to match the words with their number of syllables.

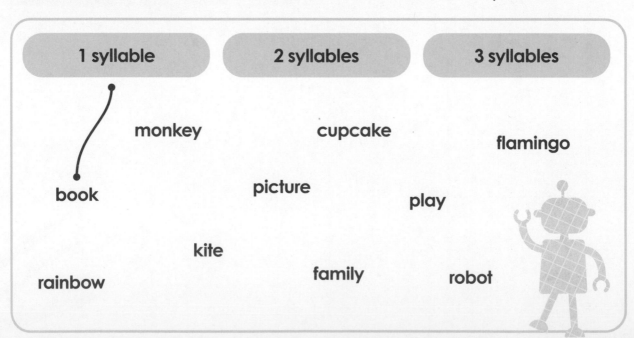

1 syllable	2 syllables	3 syllables

monkey   cupcake

                              flamingo

book

            picture
                    play

        kite

rainbow   family   robot

Vowels and Consonants

Write the correct vowel (a, e, i, o, u) in these words.

st_a_nd   sk_nk   sh_d

f_sh   dr_p

Write the correct beginning or end letter in each word.

_ent

fro_

_est

dru_

parro_

_anana

acor_

_enguin

Make as many words as you can using the letters in each grid.
You can use a letter more than once in a word.

a	g	t
f	e	d
n	h	s

....

....

....

c	i	p
t	r	o
a	d	l

....

....

....

Prefixes

A **prefix** is a group of letters added to the start of a word. It changes the word's meaning. For example, the prefix **dis–** changes **agree** to **disagree**.

The prefix **un-** means not. Circle the **un-** prefixes in **red**.
The prefix **re-** means again. Circle the **re-** prefixes in **green**.

She decided to (rewrite) her homework.

The man was unable to unlock his car.

The girl reread her favorite book many times.

The boy is unafraid of the unfriendly dog.

She unties her shoelaces and removes her shoes.

The untidy boy did not remember to recycle his trash.

Write two words for each prefix.
You can use a dictionary to help you.

Prefix	Word 1	Word 2
mis-	misbehave	
dis-		
in-		
un-		
uni-		
anti-		

Prefixes

Add a prefix to each word. You can use a prefix more than once.

re-

un-

in-

im-

dis-

non-

under-

............play

............usual

............water

............possible

............visible

............try

............appear

............wind

............sense

............stand

Complete the chart using words you did not use in the activity above. You can use a dictionary to help you.

Prefix	Meaning	Prefix + Word	Word Meaning
un-	not / change back	unlucky	to not be lucky
re-	again	re............	....
dis-	not	dis............	....
pre-	before	pre............	....
non-	not / opposite	non............	....

Suffixes

A **suffix** is a group of letters added to the end of a word. It changes the word's meaning. For example, the suffix **-ful** changes **joy** to **joyful**.

Root Word	Suffix	New Word
comfort	-able	comfortable
truth	-ful	
fear	-less	
slow	-est	
tall	-er	

Write the words in the Venn diagram to show which suffixes they can have.

care
respect
end
play
joy
enjoy
success
price
rest
watch
comfort

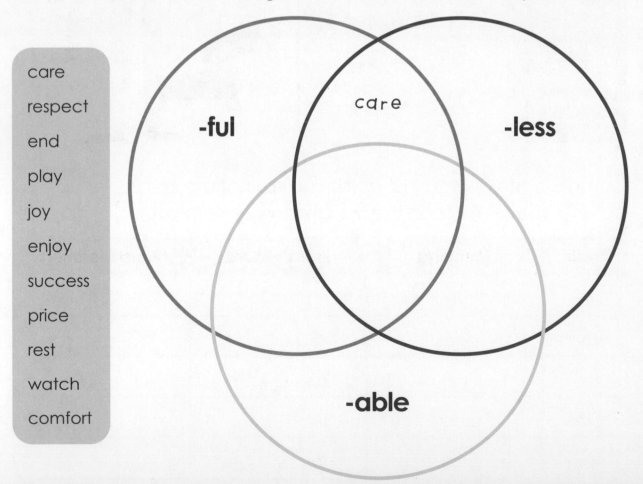

-ful   care   -less

-able

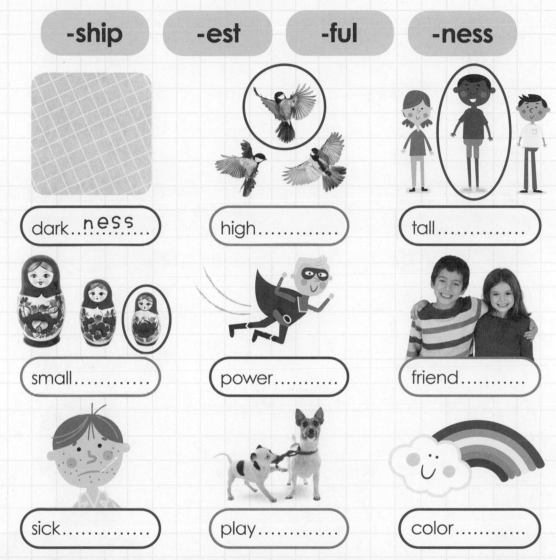

Suffixes

Match the word to the picture by adding one of these suffixes. You can use a suffix more than once.

-ship   **-est**   **-ful**   **-ness**

dark...ness...

high............

tall..............

small...........

power...........

friend...........

sick..............

play.............

color...........

Use the suffixes above in these sentences.

- The power........... rocket blasted off into space.
- Their friend........... began when they were two years old.
- The small........... dog was the most play...........
- From out of the dark........... burst color........... fireworks.

Root Words

The part of a word to which we add prefixes and suffixes is called the **root word**. **Move** is the root word of **remove** and **moving**.

Draw lines to match the words with their root words.

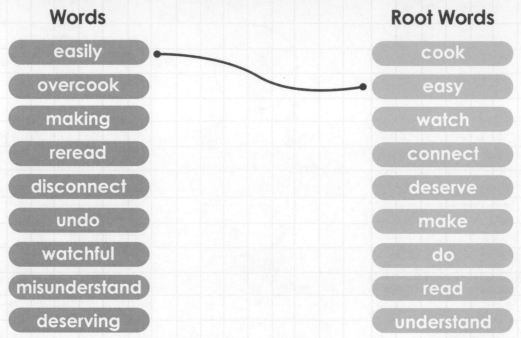

Words

- easily
- overcook
- making
- reread
- disconnect
- undo
- watchful
- misunderstand
- deserving

Root Words

- cook
- easy
- watch
- connect
- deserve
- make
- do
- read
- understand

Write the correct root word for each group.

happily
happiness
unhappy
unhappily
happiest

Root word: ..happy..

stopping
stops
nonstop
stopped
unstoppable

Root word: ....

cries
crying
outcry
cried
crier

Root word: ....

dislike
likable
likely
unlike
likes

Root word: ....

72

Compound Words

Two words joined together make a **compound word** with a new meaning.
Rain and **bow** make **rainbow**.

Draw lines to make compound words. Then circle them in the word search.

snow	stick
lip	fly
cup	hopper
grass	man
rain	cake
bed	bow
dragon	house
arm	chair
light	room
sun	flower

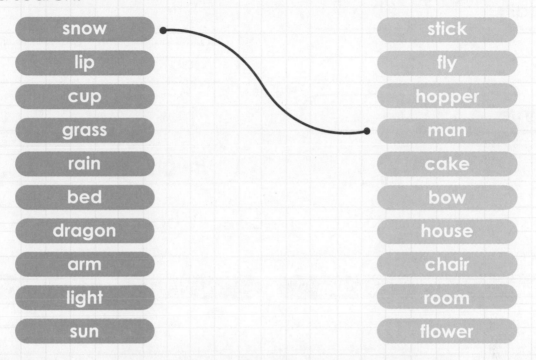

```
g b e d r o o m o n e d
r o n s u n f l o w e r
a e c a b v o i s l n a
s c a b e t c p q i w g
s s u a b s m s u g r o
h s g p i u c t a h a n
o a r m c h a i r t i f
p w e x f a h c a h n l
p e r d g h k k i o b y
e i a g o n f e b u o e
r s n o w m a n n s w l
o p d r o o f u w e y u
```

Synonyms

A **synonym** is a word that has a similar meaning to another word.
A synonym of **easy** is **simple**.

Write a synonym of each word.

talk	...speak...	little	....

begin	....	look	....

true	....	fast	....

afraid	....	laugh	....

Circle a synonym that could replace each bold word.

1 The cat was **tired** so she took a nap.

sleepy	awake	playful	hungry

2 A **big** truck zoomed past the house.

small	noisy	huge	fast

3 Ellie **loved** seeing the elephants.

disliked	adored	missed	fed

4 Max **yelled** when he stubbed his toe.

whispered	talked	walked	shouted

5 The roaring lion was very **loud**.

noisy	quiet	funny	fluffy

Antonyms

An **antonym** is a word that has the opposite meaning to another word.
An antonym of **easy** is **difficult**.

Circle the antonym of each word, and then write one more.

open	wide (close) lock	.... shut
sad	miserable scared joyful	....
slow	quick bored tired	....
quiet	noisy silent healthy	....
awake	playful loud sleeping	....
dull	fun uninteresting slowest	....

For each pair, write **A** for antonyms or **S** for synonyms.

sit stand ☐	cold chilly ☐	tiny small ☐
throw catch ☐	calm relax ☐	high low ☐
big large ☐	happy sad ☐	listen hear ☐

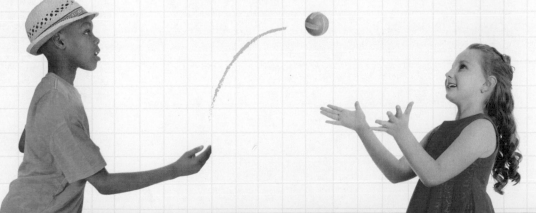

Similes

A **simile** compares two things using the words *like* or *as*.
For example, I am as brave as a lion.

Underline the correct ending to each simile.

Her shoes are as green as	the clouds	<u>the grass</u>	the sky
The light is as bright as	the sun	the dark	the night
The perfume smells as sweet as	a pizza	roses	an egg
He is as quiet as	a mouse	thunder	a truck
She swims like	a butterfly	a fish	a bird
The boy roars like	a lion	a turtle	a tree

Make up similes to complete the sentences.

My kitten is as cute as ....

The baby is as small as ....

The box is as blue as ....

She sang like ....

He galloped like ....

The puppy was soft like ....

Metaphors

A **metaphor** compares two things by saying that they are the same. For example, I am a brave lion. Metaphors do not use *like* or *as*.

Write a metaphor for each thing.

sea	The sea is a blue jewel.
cat	....
baby	....
monkey	....
snow	....

Write **metaphor** or **simile** beside each phrase.

She is as strong as an ox.	simile
My watch is as light as a feather.	....
She has a heart of gold.	....
The chocolate tastes like velvet.	....
The sisters are two peas in a pod.	....
You are a wise owl.	....
He laughs like a hyena.	....
They ran like the wind.	....
The bunny is as white as snow.	....
The clouds are fluffy marshmallows.	....

Homophones

Homophones are words that sound the same but have a different spelling and meaning.

Draw lines to match the homophones.

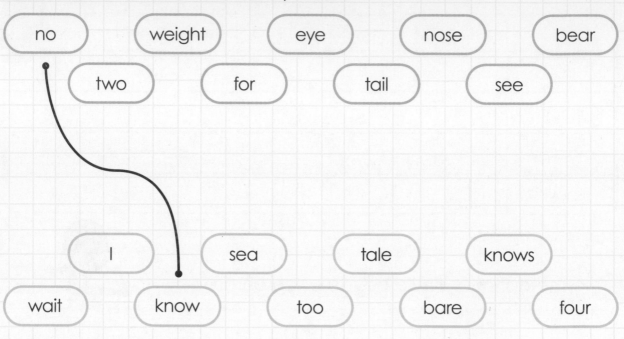

| no | weight | eye | nose | bear |
| two | | for | tail | see |

| | I | sea | tale | knows |
| wait | know | too | bare | four |

Circle the correct homophone for each sentence.
If you are unsure, use a dictionary to check.

These shirts are on **sale / sail** today.

The **bee / be** is buzzing.

She **one / won** the race.

I need a matching **pair / pear** of socks.

We use **flower / flour** to bake a cake.

Homographs

Homographs are words that have the same spelling but a different meaning. They sometimes sound different as well.

Circle the correct meaning for each bold word.

They **left** the park. (the past tense of leave) (on the left side)

The bird loved to **fly**. (a small insect) (to move in the sky)

They watched a **live** music concert. (to be alive) (something that you watch as it happens)

The puppy wore a pink **bow**. (to bend down) (a looped ribbon)

Write two meanings for each word. You can use a dictionary to help you.

Word	Meaning 1	Meaning 2
row	a group of items placed side by side	to move a boat using oars
watch		
right		
ring		
bat		

Alliteration

When we use two words together that start with the same sound, it is called **alliteration**.

Circle the two words in each row that alliterate.

(bright)	(blue)	green
loud	tiger	lion
happy	dinosaur	hippo
red	rocket	boat
playful	kitten	puppy
delicious	dessert	cupcake
dazzling	jewel	diamond
sweet	bird	smile
kind	kitten	rabbit

Underline the alliterative words in each sentence.

They saw a tiny turtle at the beach.

A careful cat crept under the fence.

The pink pig was in a muddy mess.

Flo's favorite dessert is a strawberry sundae.

Max made tasty tomato pasta.

Emotion Words

We can use **emotion words** to express how we feel.

Draw lines to match the words with the images.

 happy sad worried angry confused surprised  proud

 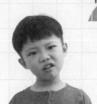 

Write how someone might feel in each situation.

Getting a new puppy	....
Going to the dentist	....
Visiting family or a friend	....
Winning a prize	....
Placing last in a sports tournament	....
Learning a new language	....
If a favorite toy goes missing	....

Write three things or events that make you feel happy.

1 ....

2 ....

3 ....

Dictionary Practice

A **dictionary** tells us the spelling and meaning of a word. It also tells us what type of word it is, such as a noun. The words are listed in alphabetical order.

Use a dictionary to find the meanings of these words. Then use each word in a sentence.

Word	Meaning	Sentence
prehistoric	a time before written records	Dinosaurs are prehistoric animals.
inquisitive		
melancholy		
exterior		
resemble		

Use a dictionary to find a word that fits each description.

An adjective (describing word) beginning with **a**: ....

An adjective beginning with **t**: ....

A verb (doing word) beginning with **d**: ....

A verb beginning with **p**: ....

A noun (naming word) beginning with **s**: ....

A noun beginning with **f**: ....

Glossary Practice

A **glossary** is a section at the back of a nonfiction book that gives you the meanings of key words used in the book.

Read each paragraph and circle the words found in the glossary.

Dinosaurs roamed the Earth more than 66 million years ago. Some were herbivores, and others were carnivores. Today, scientists study fossils to find out more about how dinosaurs lived.

Glossary

carnivore: a meat-eating animal

fossil: the remains of a living thing that have changed into rock over many years

herbivore: a plant-eating animal

Use a dictionary to help you write glossary definitions for the words in bold type.

A volcano **erupts** when the plates that make up the Earth's crust slide over each other. Hot **liquid magma** rises to the **surface**, where it is called **lava**. The **lava** either explodes into the sky or flows over the ground. Gradually, it cools and hardens into solid rock.

Glossary

erupt: ....

lava: ....

liquid: ....

magma: ....

surface: ....

The Subject

The **subject** of a sentence is the main person, animal, or thing that the sentence is about. The rest of the sentence gives information about the subject.

Write the correct subject into each sentence.

> That oak tree   **my class**   A bird   **Their family**   our teacher   **Tim and Tom**

1 .....A bird..... is chirping outside my window.

2 .... are twin brothers.

3 Tomorrow, ... is going on a field trip.

4 .... has many acorns on it this year.

5 Today, ... taught us about fractions.

6 .... went on a vacation to Mexico.

Circle the subject of each sentence.

1 Today, (Julia) gave Sid a dog biscuit.

2 Yesterday, Tom went to visit his grandma.

3 My parents cleaned out the garage.

4 This building is the tallest building in town.

5 I am already on level six of this game.

6 *T. rex* was a fast-running, meat-eating dinosaur.

Irregular Plurals

Nouns are naming words. Most nouns form their plural by adding –s. For example, cat becomes cats.

Irregular nouns, however, form their plurals in other ways.

Write the plurals of these words that end in a **consonant** and the letter **-y**. Drop the **-y** and add **-ies**.

one **pony**	two ......ponies......		one **baby**	two ....
one **story**	two		one **family**	two ....
one **fly**	two		one **city**	two ....

Write the plurals of these words that end in **-ss**, **-sh**, **-ch**, and **-x**. Add **-es** to each word.

one **fox**	two ......foxes......		one **dress**	two ....
one **dish**	two		one **lunch**	two ....
one **boss**	two		one **box**	two ....

Write the plurals of these words that end in **-f** or **-fe**. Drop the **-f** or **-fe** and add **-ves**.

one **leaf**	two ......leaves......		one **shelf**	two ....
one **wife**	two		one **loaf**	two ....
one **life**	two		one **half**	two ....

Irregular Plurals

Some **irregular plurals** don't follow a rule. You just need to learn these words.

Draw lines to match the singular phrases with the plural phrases.

Singular	Plural
one mouse	two people
one tooth	two women
one child	two geese
one person	two sheep
one deer	two children
one goose	two fungi
one man	two fish
one sheep	two mice
one woman	two men
one foot	two deer
one fish	two teeth
one fungus	two feet

Proper Nouns

Names, places, special occasions, days of the week, and months are **proper nouns**.

They always begin with a capital letter.

Circle the proper noun in each group.

1   cat   kitty   (Max)   **2**   girl   Emily   sister

3   state   Texas   south   **4**   Friday   today   now

5   birthday   New Year   party   **6**   summer   hot   July

Write a proper noun in the spaces below. Remember to use capital letters.

1 The street I live on is called ....Chestnut Road..........

2 I was born in the month of ....

3 Both Tuesday and .... begin with T.

4 My family likes to celebrate

....

5 The city nearest my home is

....

6 A good name for a dog is

....

Past Tense

Text that is in the **past tense** is about things that have already happened.

Regular verbs end in **-ed** when they are in the past tense.
Circle the verbs that are in the past tense.

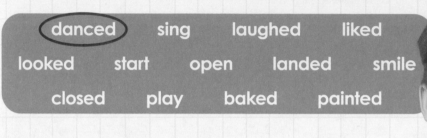

(danced)   sing   laughed   liked

looked   start   open   landed   smile

closed   play   baked   painted

Rewrite each sentence, changing the **bold** verb into the past tense.

1 She **helps** her brother read his book.

...... She helped her brother read his book ......

2 My mom **arrives** to pick us up.

....

3 Riley **kicks** the ball into the goal.

....

4 I **ask** my dad to help me build a treehouse.

....

5 We **look** everywhere for Jo's lost glasses.

....

6 He **crosses** the road to get to the park.

....

Future Tense

Text that is in the **future tense** is about things that might happen in the future.

We use the word *will* to form the future tense. Use *will* and the verb in brackets to complete each sentence in the future tense.

1 In July, Pippa ...will visit... her friends in Canada. **(visit)**

2 Tomorrow, we .... a train into town. **(catch)**

3 This afternoon, I .... for a swim. **(go)**

4 Next year, Ben .... school. **(start)**

5 I think Scarlett .... at my joke. **(laugh)**

6 They .... horses every day at camp. **(ride)**

Write about the things you'd like to do when you grow up.

When I grow up, I will ....

....

....

....

....

....

....

....

Past, Present, and Future

We use **verbs**, or doing words, to tell the reader whether something happened in the past, is happening now, or will happen in the future.

Fill in the gaps in this verb chart.

Past Tense	Present Tense	Future Tense
asked	............ask............	will ask
called	....	will call
....	love	will love
talked	....	....
....	move	....

Decide if each sentence is in the past, present, or future tense, and circle the correct word.

1 We listen to music in the car.   past   (present)   future

We listened to music in the car.   past   present   future

We will listen to music in the car.   past   present   future

2 They picked their favorite flavors.   past   present   future

They will pick their favorite flavors.   past   present   future

They pick their favorite flavors.   past   present   future

3 The dog will rest on the mat.   past   present   future

The dog rests on the mat.   past   present   future

The dog rested on the mat.   past   present   future

4 Our cat stretched out by the fire.   past   present   future

Our cat will stretch out by the fire.   past   present   future

Our cat stretches out by the fire.   past   present   future

Irregular Verbs

Most **verbs** form their past tense by adding –ed.

Irregular verbs, however, form their past tense in other ways.

Write the past-tense form of these verbs. Drop the **-y** and add **-ied**.

cry .....cried.....	fry ....
spy	copy ....
try	reply ....

Write the correct past-tense form of the verb in each sentence.

ran   **found**   took   **won**   made   **went**   drew   **wrote**   did   **slept**

Present Tense	Past Tense
1 I take a book from the shelf.	I .....took..... a book from the shelf.
2 She draws a picture.	She .... a picture.
3 He goes to school.	He .... to school.
4 I find my lost watch.	I .... my lost watch.
5 Ellie writes a funny story.	Ellie .... a funny story.
6 I sleep through the storm.	I .... through the storm.
7 Mike wins first prize.	Mike .... first prize.
8 They make their beds.	They .... their beds.
9 We run as fast as we can.	We .... as fast as we could.
10 What do you want to watch?	What .... you watch yesterday?

Adjectives

Adjectives describe nouns. *Happy* and *short* are adjectives.

Write the adjectives in the correct place in each sentence.

1 Our ....greedy.... dog ate
.....two..... burgers.

two greedy

2 A .... superhero
rescued the .... baby.

tiny brave

3 The .... man
dropped the .... vase.

clumsy glass

4 I put ....
sandwiches in my lunch box.

cheese two

5 The .... audience couldn't
hear the singer's .... voice.

noisy quiet

6 The .... hall was full of
.... children.

excited crowded

Write a sentence using both adjectives.

1 four, huge: ....

2 lazy, muddy: ....

3 talented, fast: ....

4 early, hungry: ....

5 blue, sparkling: ....

6 happy, tall: ....

Adverbs

Adverbs add to verbs. They tell us *when*, *where*, or *how* something happens.

Many adverbs end in **-ly**. Write an adverb in each sentence.

quickly	loudly	**carefully**	bravely	**accidentally**	peacefully

1 He ...accidentally.. dropped his ice-cream cone.

2 I cheered .... when my team came onto the field.

3 He carried the full tray .... across the room.

4 She .... rescued the baby from the fire.

5 Mia .... ran to a tree for shelter.

6 The dog is sleeping .... in his bed.

Circle *when*, *where*, or *how* to say what sort of information each adverb gives us.

before	(when)	where	how
here	when	where	how
gently	when	where	how
yesterday	when	where	how
outside	when	where	how
soon	when	where	how
quietly	when	where	how
today	when	where	how
everywhere	when	where	how
later	when	where	how

Connectives

Connectives are words that we use to connect, or join, two sentences together.

Use one of these words to join each pair of sentences.
You can use the same word more than once.

so   **and**   because   **then**   but

1 He did his homework. He forgot to take it back to school.

He did his homework, but he forgot to take it back to school.

2 Olivia did her homework straight away. She watched TV.

....

3 I like carrots and peas. I don't like cauliflower.

....

4 Madison worked hard. Her mom gave her a reward.

....

5 Noah was happy. His friends were coming to visit.

....

6 We went swimming. We rode our bikes.

....

7 First, I fed the dog. I took him for a walk.

....

8 She wore a coat. It was cold.

....

Reflexive Pronouns

Reflexive pronouns refer back to the subject of the verb.

They are: myself, yourself, herself, himself, itself, ourselves, yourselves, themselves.

Circle the **subject** of each sentence in **blue**, and circle the **reflexive pronoun** in **green**.

1 The children made dinner for themselves.

2 Mike bought himself some new sneakers.

3 You must behave yourselves today.

4 We are teaching ourselves to skateboard.

5 The wild beast saw itself in the mirror.

6 After losing the race, she felt sorry for herself.

Write the correct reflexive pronoun into each sentence.

1 The door appeared to open by ....

2 The rabbits went back into their hutch by ....

3 Tom and I cleaned the house by ....

4 Lucy burned .... on the hot pan.

5 I made this gift all by ....

6 After his swim, Matt dried .... well.

Rearranging Sentences

We can move parts of sentences, or phrases, to different positions.

Move the phrase at the start of each sentence to the end.

1 To learn to cook, I went to cooking classes.

I went to cooking classes to learn to cook.

2 By his chair, you will find his faithful dog.

....

3 On tiptoes, we crept past the sleeping baby.

....

4 Every morning, my mom goes for a run.

....

Move the phrase at the end of each sentence
to the start. Add a comma after the phrase.

1 I always take a shower at the start of the day.

At the start of the day, I always take a shower.

2 We started hiking at daybreak.

....

3 We saw some deer in the forest.

....

4 Always wear a helmet when riding your bike.

....

Active and Passive

In an **active sentence**, the subject does something.

In a **passive sentence**, something is done to the subject.

Rewrite each passive sentence as an active sentence. Start with the person who does the action.

1 The cat was fed by Mrs. Green.

Mrs. Green ....*fed the cat*......

2 The door was shut by the teacher.

The teacher ....

3 The book was read by Emily.

Emily ....

4 Our play was seen by many people.

Many people ....

5 The cake was baked by Harry.

Harry ....

6 The UFO was flown by a green alien.

A green alien ....

7 The mouse was watched by the cat.

The cat ....

8 The ball was thrown into the hoop by Joe.

Joe ....

Three Ways to Finish

End questions with a **question mark**.

End short sentences about surprising or important things with an **exclamation mark**.

End all other sentences with **periods**.

Add a period, a question mark, and an exclamation mark to each set of sentences.

1 Wow, a lion **!**

Is that a lion **?**

There is a lion at the zoo **.**

2 Are you able to help me ☐

Help me ☐

I would like you to help me ☐

3 What a mess ☐

This room is very messy ☐

Why is this room such a mess ☐

4 I think a bug has bitten me ☐

Has a bug bitten me ☐

Ouch ☐

5 How exciting ☐

I feel excited about it ☐

Are you excited, too ☐

6 Are you free to come over here ☐

I would like it if you came over here ☐

Come here ☐

Write a question, an exclamation, and an ordinary sentence. Use the word *stop* in each sentence.

Exclamation:

....

Question:

....

Ordinary sentence:

....

Contractions

A **contraction** is two words joined together.

We use an **apostrophe** to replace the missing letters.

Write the two words that make up each contraction.

what's	....what....	....is....
you're	....	....
I'm	....	....
they'll	....	....
can't	....	....
we've	....	....

Write the contractions for these words.

let us	.....let's.....
are not	....
I will	....
we are	....
it is	....
I have	....

Possessive Apostrophes

We use **apostrophes** to show that someone owns something.

Instead of saying *the car belonging to the man*, we can say *the man's car*.

Rewrite the possessive phrases using an apostrophe and the letter -s.

the bed belonging to the dog	the dog's bed
the house belonging to the woman	
the nose belonging to the boy	
the ideas belonging to Sophie	
the handle belonging to the bag	
the cake belonging to Harry	

Circle the correct word for each sentence. Use an apostrophe to show ownership. Do not use an apostrophe to show two of something.

1 Two (cats) / cat's live across the road.

The cats / (cat's) food is in his bowl.

2 The books / book's cover is ripped.

The books / book's are over there.

3 The singers / singer's are ready for the show.

The singers / singer's voice is very loud.

4 The dinosaurs / dinosaur's baby hatched from an egg.

The dinosaurs / dinosaur's lived long ago.

Possessive Apostrophes

To make most **plural nouns** possessive, just add an apostrophe.

If an **irregular plural** doesn't already end in –s, add an apostrophe and an –s.

Add apostrophes to make these plurals possessive.

the rabbits' noses	the carrots tops
the horses tails	the trucks horns
the monsters fur	the writers stories
the boys wishes	the crabs claws
the babies rattles	the bosses offices

Add an apostrophe and the letter -s to each irregular plural.

the men's jackets	the women team
the children bikes	the mice cheese
the teeth cavities	the people homes
the fungi colors	the cacti spines
the geese eggs	the sheep wool

Where I live

Spell each word aloud. Then write it, cover it, and write it again.

Spell it aloud.	Write it.	Practice it.
door	....	....
window	....	....
house	....	....
yard	....	....
street	....	....
town	....	....
city	....	....

Read the story about Ella's house and fill in the missing words.

Ella lives in a yellow .... with a green front ....

The house has arched .... and a tree in the ....

She lives on a quiet .... in a small ....

Opposites

Read the words on the left, and then unscramble the letters on the right to reveal their opposites.

before	fatre	....
hot	dloc	....
wrong	gitrh	....
first	tals	....
open	socle	....

Spell each word aloud, and then write it, cover it, and write it again.

Spell it aloud.	Write it.	Practice it.
first	....	....
last	....	....
before	....	....
after	....	....
hot	....	....
cold	....	....
wrong	....	....
right	....	....
open	....	....
close	....	....

Position Words

Spell each word aloud. Then write it, cover it, and write it again.

Spell it aloud.	Write it.	Practice it.
over	....	....
under	....	....
above	....	....
below	....	....
inside	....	....
outside	....	....
between	....	....
behind	....	....

Underline the position words in the sentences below. Some have more than one.

The rabbit squeezed under the fence to get inside the garden.

The spider crawled behind the curtain.

The dolls are kept above the books.

"Let's go inside," said Fran. "It's too hot outside."

Our car is parked between the red and the blue car.

Rainbow Words

Finish coloring the words, and then spell them aloud, cover them, and write them again.

red	orange	black
yellow	purple	brown
blue	green	pink

Fill in the color words on the rainbow.

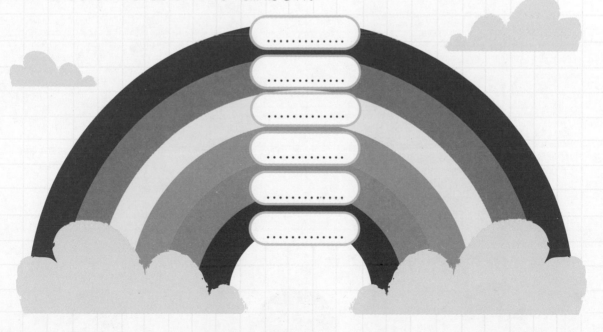

What is your favorite color and why? ....

....

Number Words

Circle the letters to spell each word. Then write the word, cover it, and write it again.

		Write it.	Practice it.
one	o t l b n a k r e s		
two	e c t o q x w o n s		
three	t i h m r l e h b e		
four	v o f i l o r u r		
five	f e i n v o a l e p		
six	z j s a q i c k x e		
seven	s a e v o e m n y		
eight	a e c i y g u h n t		
nine	n a y i o w n x e l		
ten	h o l t e m u n a		

Tricky Words

Spell each word aloud. Then write it, cover it, and write it again.

Spell it aloud.	Write it.	Practice it.
pretty		
because		
clothes		
great		
children		
something		
every		
quiet		

Circle the word that is spelled correctly in each row and rewrite it.

always	always	allways	alwas	....
does	dos	doos	does	....
together	togever	together	tugevver	....
where	wher	wehre	where	....
people	people	peeple	poelpe	....
anything	ennything	annthing	anything	....

Silent Letters

These words all have silent letters. Circle the silent letter, and then write the word, cover it, and write it again.

Spell it aloud.	Write it.	Practice it.
climb	....	....
write	....	....
gnat	....	....
knee	....	....
comb	....	....
knife	....	....
gnaw	....	....
crumb	....	....

Write a sentence using at least two of the words above.

....

....

....

....

....

....

....

Emotion Words

Spell each word aloud. Then write it, cover it, and write it again.

Spell it aloud.	Write it.	Practice it.
happy	....	....
sad	....	....
bored	....	....
angry	....	....
afraid	....	....
excited	....	....
surprised	....	....
worried	....	....

Find the emotion words in the word search.

happy
sad
bored
angry
afraid
excited
surprised
worried

r	g	b	e	y	a	l	w	w	a
a	s	e	o	x	s	n	x	o	f
b	o	r	e	d	c	c	s	r	r
e	h	a	p	p	y	i	d	r	a
s	w	c	m	e	h	i	t	i	i
b	a	h	i	t	a	s	l	e	d
t	e	d	n	q	g	h	u	d	d
s	u	r	p	r	i	s	e	d	i
a	o	s	y	r	t	f	e	c	s
a	n	g	r	y	a	b	y	i	r

How do you feel today? Choose a spelling word from above or use your own.

....

....

....

Family Words

Spell each word aloud. Then write it, cover it, and write it again.

Spell it aloud.	Write it.	Practice it.
brother	....	....
sister	....	....
aunt	....	....
uncle	....	....
nephew	....	....
niece	....	....
cousin	....	....
grandmother	....	....
grandfather	....	....

Who is in your family? Write their names below.

....
....
....
....
....
....

Days of the Week

Fill in the missing vowels (a, e, i, o, u) to complete the days of the week. Then write them in full, cover them, and write them again.

Day	Write it.	Practice it.
M__nd__y	....	....
T__ __sd__y	....	....
W__ dn __ sd__y	....	....
Th__ rsd__y	....	....
Fr__ d__y	....	....
S__ t__rd__y	....	....
S__nd__y	....	....

Add the missing days of the week to the diary.

August

....

....

....

....Tuesday....

....Saturday....

...Wednesday..

....

Season Words

Spell each word aloud. Then write it, cover it, and write it again.

Spell it aloud.	Write it.	Practice it.
season	....	....
spring	....	....
summer	....	....
fall	....	....
winter	....	....
year	....	....

Circle the correct spelling in each row, and then rewrite the word.

saison   seeson   season   ....

sume   summer   somer   ....

year   yare   yeer   ....

winter   winntar   wineter   ....

spring   sringe   sprig   ....

fawl   fale   fall   ....

Travel Words

Find the travel words in the word search below.

world	r w b e y a p w s r
suitcase	a s o o g s l x o q
plane	b v e r j t a h t n
boat	e h z k l a n o r a
train	w w c f e d e t i l
hotel	s u i t c a s e n d
tickets	t e d w t g t l d m
taxi	s u r b o a t a d i
	t i c k e t s n x s
	t r a i n a b k i i

Spell each word aloud. Then write it, cover it, and write it again.

Spell it aloud.	Write It.	Practice it.
world	....	....
suitcase	....	....
plane	....	....
boat	....	....
train	....	....
hotel	....	....
tickets	....	....
taxi	....	....

Weather Words

Spell each word aloud. Then write it, cover it, and write it again.

Spell it aloud.	Write it.	Practice it.
cloudy	....	....
rainy	....	....
sunny	....	....
snowy	....	....
windy	....	....
hot	....	....
cold	....	....

Write a word under each image to describe the weather.

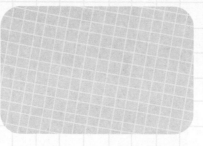

....

....

114

Compound Words

Write the correct words under each image to make the compound words.

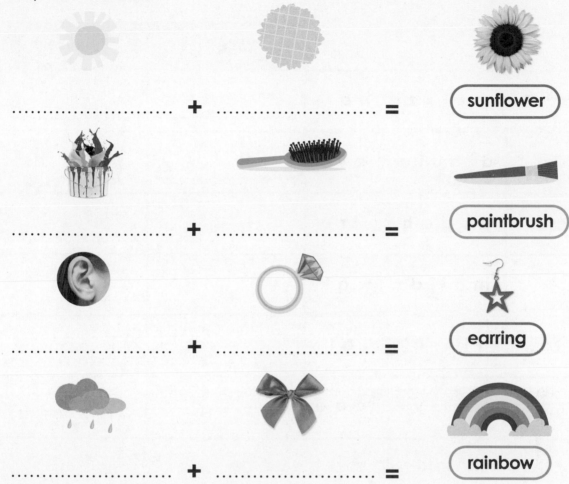

.... + ... = (sunflower)

.... + ... = (paintbrush)

.... + ... = (earring)

.... + ... = (rainbow)

Spell each word aloud. Then write it, cover it, and write it again.

Spell it aloud.	Write it.	Practice it.
sunflower	....	....
paintbrush	....	....
earring	....	....
rainbow	....	....

Food Words

Circle the letters to spell each word. Then write the word, cover it, and write it again.

		Write it.	Practice it.
pizza	p e i x z r z n a r	....	....
juice	d j o u i a m c v e	....	....
pasta	p u g a h s e t r a	....	....
milk	m u j i d n l w q k	....	....
fruit	r f v r o o u i a t	....	....
bread	c h b r y e o c a d	....	....

Find and link the letters to spell the words.

pizza ☐   juice ☐   pasta ☐   milk ☐   fruit ☐   bread ☐

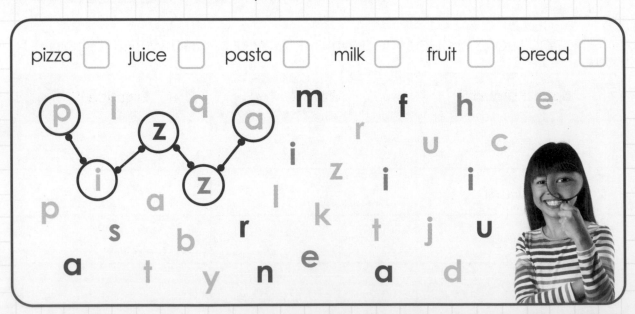

The Suffix -tion

Spell each word aloud. Then write it, cover it, and write it again.

Spell it aloud.	Write it.	Practice it.
station		
action		
fraction		
direction		
information		
motion		
question		
invitation		

Use the words with -tion endings to complete the sentences below.

The train pulled slowly into the ....

Let's go to the library to find some more ....

He pressed the button to set the car in ....

Can you repeat the ...., please?

The birthday party .... arrived in the mail.

Which .... is it, north or south?

Irregular Verbs

Circle the correct past-tense verb and write it in the sentence.

swim swam	Last week, we .... in the swimming pool.
see saw	I .... him at school yesterday.
hear heard	The children .... a strange sound coming from the kitchen.
did do	Noah .... not like his noodles.
slept sleep	In the tent, Caleb .... in his sleeping bag.
make made	I .... you a birthday card.
gave give	Emma .... her friend a hug.

Spell each word aloud. Then write it, cover it, and write it again.

Spell it aloud.	Write it.	Practice it.
swam	....	....
saw	....	....
heard	....	....
did	....	....
wrote	....	....
slept	....	....
made	....	....
gave	....	....

Sight Words

Circle the correct spelling in each row, and then rewrite the word.

both	**buth**	**bouth**	**both**	....
don't	**do'nt**	**don't**	**donnt**	....
found	**foand**	**foind**	**found**	....
made	**maid**	**maed**	**made**	....
very	**very**	**verry**	**verey**	....
would	**wood**	**woald**	**would**	....
write	**wriet**	**write**	**rite**	....
wait	**wait**	**wayt**	**waet**	....

Spell each word aloud. Then write it, cover it, and write it again.

Spell it aloud.	Write it.	Practice it.
begin	....	....
those	....	....
upon	....	....
use	....	....
buy	....	....
call	....	....
many	....	....
best	....	....

10 Tens is 100

1 The number 100 is made of 10 tens. Trace the number sentence.

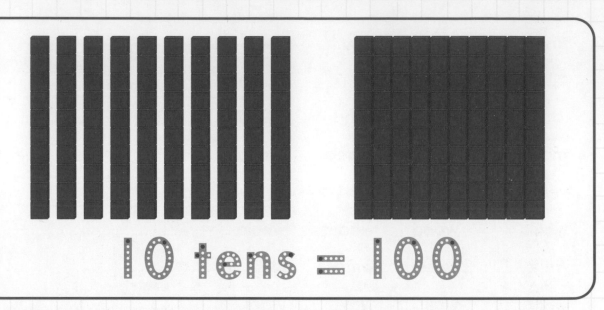

10 tens = 100

2 Circle ten groups of ten to show 100 ladybugs.

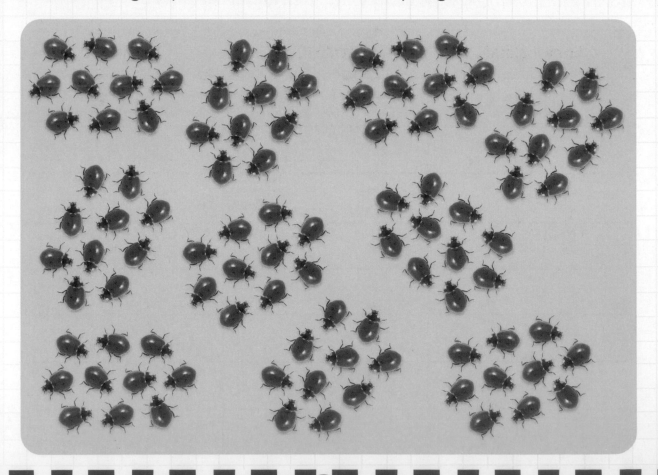

Adding 100s

1 The number 300 is made of 3 hundreds.
Trace the number sentence.

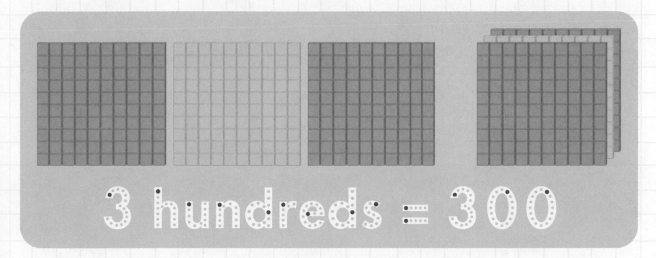

3 hundreds = 300

2 Count the hundreds blocks to solve the problems.

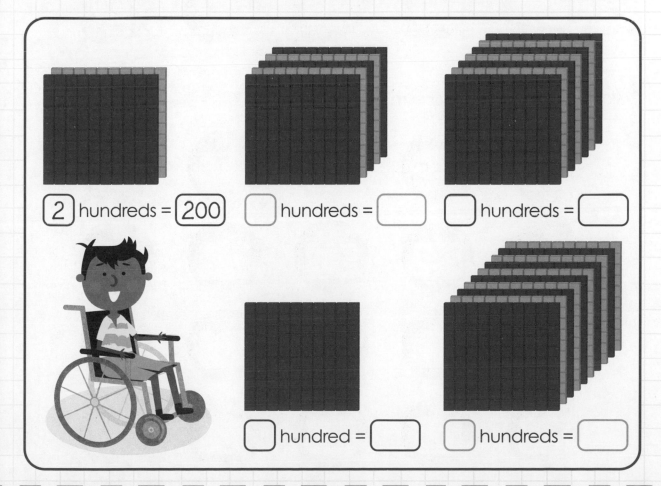

2 hundreds = 200

☐ hundreds = ☐

☐ hundreds = ☐

☐ hundred = ☐

☐ hundreds = ☐

Skip Counting by 5's

1 Skip count by 5's. Start at 105.

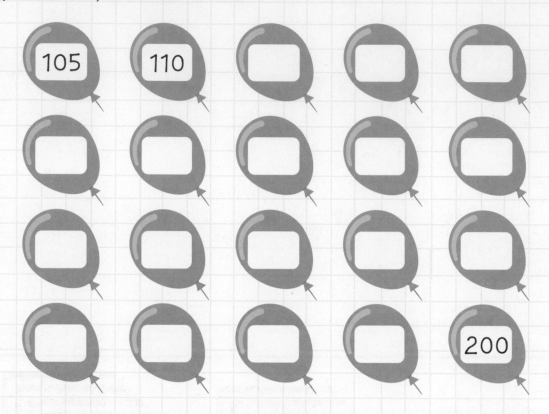

105   110   [ ]   [ ]   [ ]

[ ]   [ ]   [ ]   [ ]   [ ]

[ ]   [ ]   [ ]   [ ]   [ ]

[ ]   [ ]   [ ]   [ ]   200

2 Skip count by 5's. Start at 350.

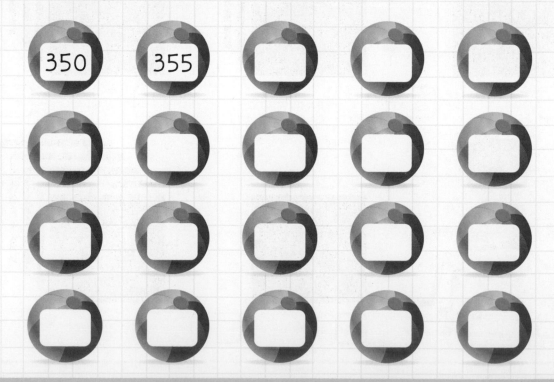

350   355   [ ]   [ ]   [ ]

[ ]   [ ]   [ ]   [ ]   [ ]

[ ]   [ ]   [ ]   [ ]   [ ]

[ ]   [ ]   [ ]   [ ]   [ ]

Skip Counting by 10's

1 Skip count by 10's. Start at 200.

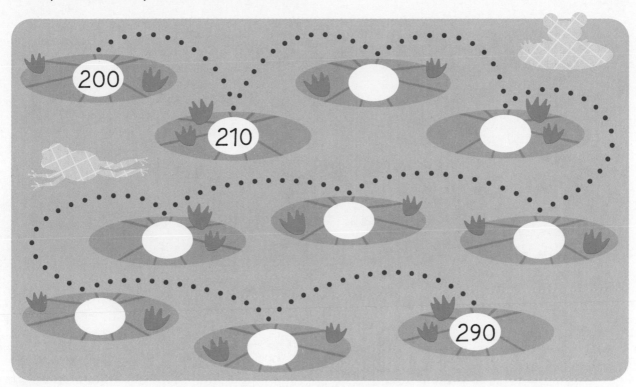

2 Skip count by 10's. Start at 450.

Skip Counting by 100's

1 10 hundreds is 1000. Trace the number sentence.

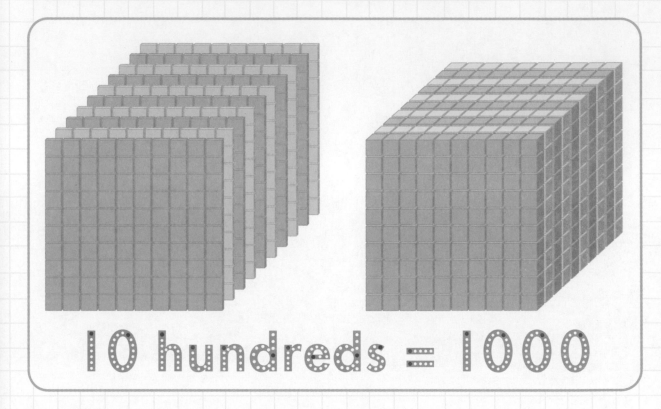

10 hundreds = 1000

2 Skip count by 100's up to 1000.

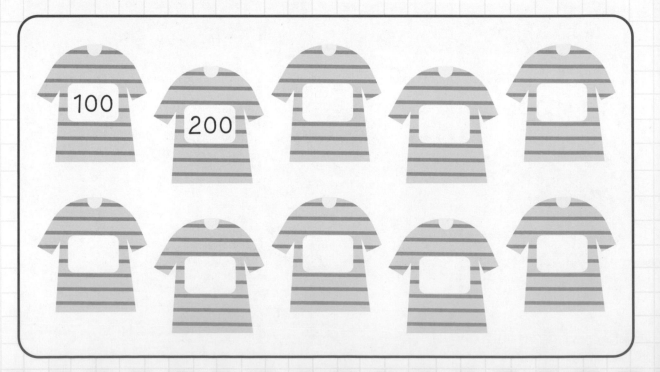

100 200

Adding 10's and 1's

Count the packs of 10 and the ones to solve the problems.

4 tens + 3 ones = 43

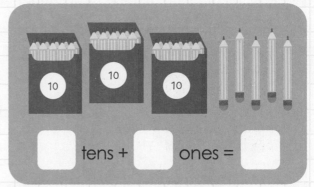

___ tens + ___ ones = ___

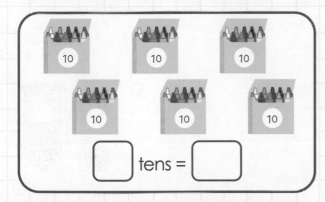

___ tens + ___ ones = ___

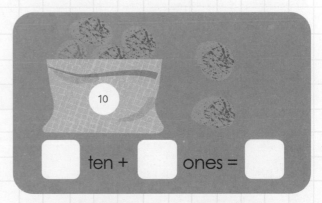

___ tens + ___ ones = ___

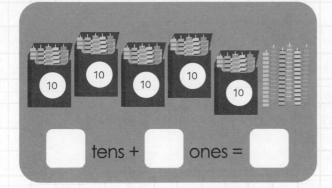

___ tens = ___

___ ten + ___ ones = ___

___ tens + ___ ones = ___

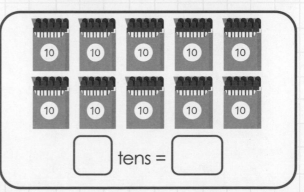

___ tens = ___

100's, 10's, and 1's

Count the hundreds, tens, and ones to figure out how many units there are altogether.

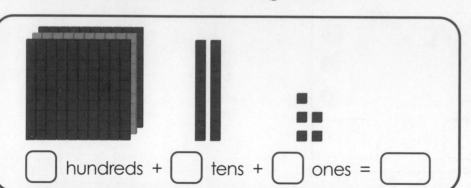

⬜ hundreds + ⬜ tens + ⬜ ones = ⬜

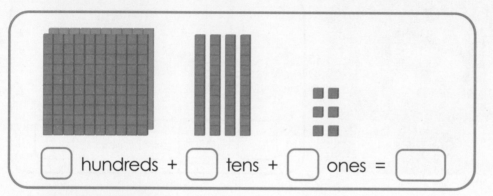

⬜ hundreds + ⬜ tens + ⬜ ones = ⬜

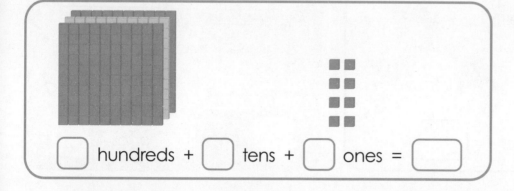

⬜ hundreds + ⬜ tens + ⬜ ones = ⬜

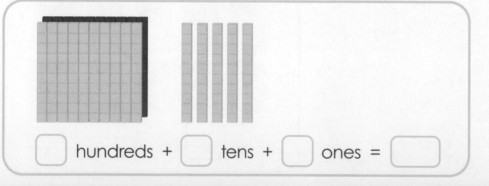

⬜ hundreds + ⬜ tens + ⬜ ones = ⬜

Place Value

Look at each number, and then write each digit under its place value in the chart.

	hundreds	tens	ones
473	4	7	3
826			
555			
321			
835			
840			
911			
702			
663			
900			

100's, 10's, or 1's?

Write the digit that is in each place.

583

[8] is in the tens place.

[5] is in the hundreds place.

[3] is in the ones place.

734

[ ] is in the ones place.

[ ] is in the hundreds place.

[ ] is in the tens place.

462

[ ] is in the hundreds place.

[ ] is in the ones place.

[ ] is in the tens place.

614

[ ] is in the hundreds place.

[ ] is in the tens place.

[ ] is in the ones place.

570

[ ] is in the ones place.

[ ] is in the tens place.

[ ] is in the hundreds place.

361

[ ] is in the hundreds place.

[ ] is in the ones place.

[ ] is in the tens place.

908

[ ] is in the tens place.

[ ] is in the hundreds place.

[ ] is in the ones place.

800

[ ] is in the hundreds place.

[ ] is in the tens place.

[ ] is in the ones place.

100's, 10's, or 1's?

For each underlined digit, write hundreds, tens, or ones in the place-value column. Then write the digit's value in the value column.

	Place Value	Value
<u>5</u>27	hundreds	500
7<u>3</u>4		
82<u>4</u>		
4<u>7</u>5		
60<u>3</u>		
<u>9</u>83		
2<u>6</u>0		
14<u>2</u>		
<u>3</u>72		
8<u>0</u>4		

Working With 10

1 Use the hundred chart to help
you add or subtract 10.

1	2	3	4	5	6	7	8	9	10
11	12	13	14	15	16	17	18	19	20
21	22	23	24	25	26	27	28	29	30
31	32	33	34	35	36	37	38	39	40
41	42	43	44	45	46	47	48	49	50
51	52	53	54	55	56	57	58	59	60
61	62	63	64	65	66	67	68	69	70
71	72	73	74	75	76	77	78	79	80
81	82	83	84	85	86	87	88	89	90
91	92	93	94	95	96	97	98	99	100

23 + 10 = 33   32 + 10 = ☐   89 + 10 = ☐

15 + 10 = ☐   40 + 10 = ☐   74 + 10 = ☐

60 – 10 = ☐   46 – 10 = ☐   77 – 10 = ☐

53 – 10 = ☐   99 – 10 = ☐   65 – 10 = ☐

2 Fill in the missing numbers.

35 + ☐ = 45   ☐ + 10 = 63   10 + ☐ = 52

71 – ☐ = 61   ☐ – 10 = 83   ☐ – 10 = 48

Working With 10

Add 10 to solve the problems.

150 + 10 = ☐   237 + 10 = ☐   542 + 10 = ☐

735 + 10 = ☐   989 + 10 = ☐   374 + 10 = ☐

100 + 10 = ☐   401 + 10 = ☐   190 + 10 = ☐

590 + 10 = ☐   600 + 10 = ☐   990 + 10 = ☐

Subtract 10 to solve the problems.

482 − 10 = ☐   734 − 10 = ☐   827 − 10 = ☐

227 − 10 = ☐   565 − 10 = ☐   379 − 10 = ☐

100 − 10 = ☐   205 − 10 = ☐   670 − 10 = ☐

901 − 10 = ☐   400 − 10 = ☐   1000 − 10 = ☐

How Much Is 400?

1 Fill in the gaps in the sentences.

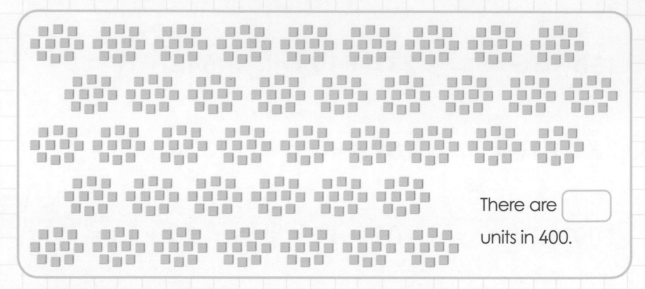

There are ☐ units in 400.

We can swap each group of ten units for a tens rod.

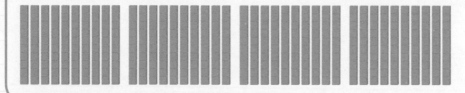

There are ☐ tens in 400.

We can swap each group of 10 tens rods for a hundred square.

There are ☐ hundreds in 400.

2 Cross out the two incorrect words in each sentence.

Counting to 400 in **ones / tens / hundreds** takes the longest time.

The quickest way to count to 400 is to count in **ones / tens / hundreds**.

Naming Numbers

Match the numerals with their number names.

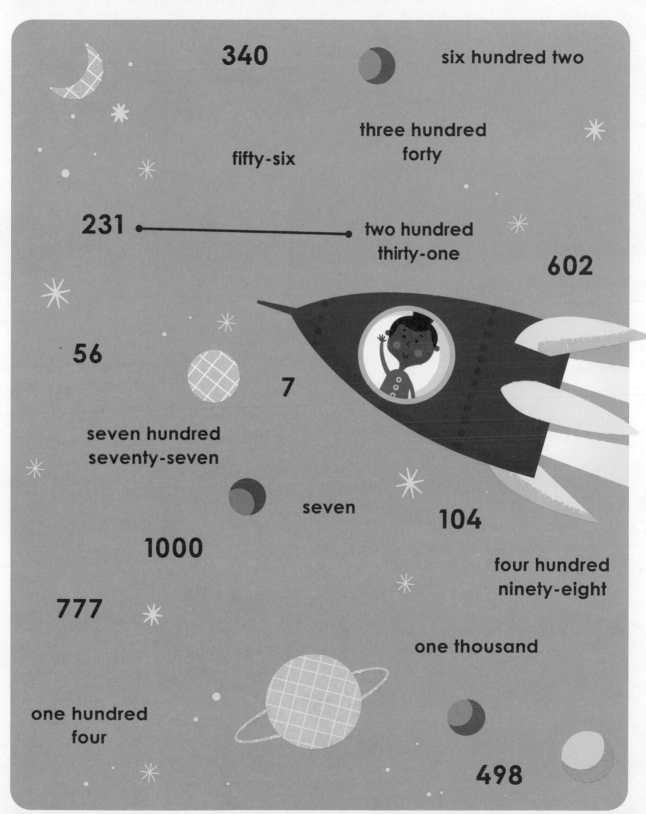

340

six hundred two

three hundred forty

fifty-six

231 ———————————— two hundred thirty-one

602

56

7

seven hundred seventy-seven

seven

104

1000

four hundred ninety-eight

777

one thousand

one hundred four

498

Number Names

1 Write the numbers using numerals.

five hundred seventeen	517
three hundred twenty-five	
six hundred twelve	
one thousand	
two hundred six	
eight hundred forty	

2 Write the numbers using words.

282	two hundred eighty-two
524	
603	
714	
830	
1000	

Expanded Form

1 Add the hundreds, tens, and ones to solve the problems.

$600 + 30 + 2 = \boxed{632}$ $400 + 10 + 5 = \boxed{}$

$200 + 50 + 1 = \boxed{}$ $700 + 60 + 9 = \boxed{}$

$900 + 90 = \boxed{}$ $300 + 4 = \boxed{}$

2 Write the numbers in expanded form.

$834 = \boxed{800} + \boxed{30} + \boxed{4}$ $244 = \boxed{} + \boxed{} + \boxed{}$

$618 = \boxed{} + \boxed{} + \boxed{}$ $735 = \boxed{} + \boxed{} + \boxed{}$

$470 = \boxed{} + \boxed{}$ $205 = \boxed{} + \boxed{}$

Compare Numbers

Write the numbers shown. Then write **<** (less than), **>** (greater than), or **=** (equals) between each pair.

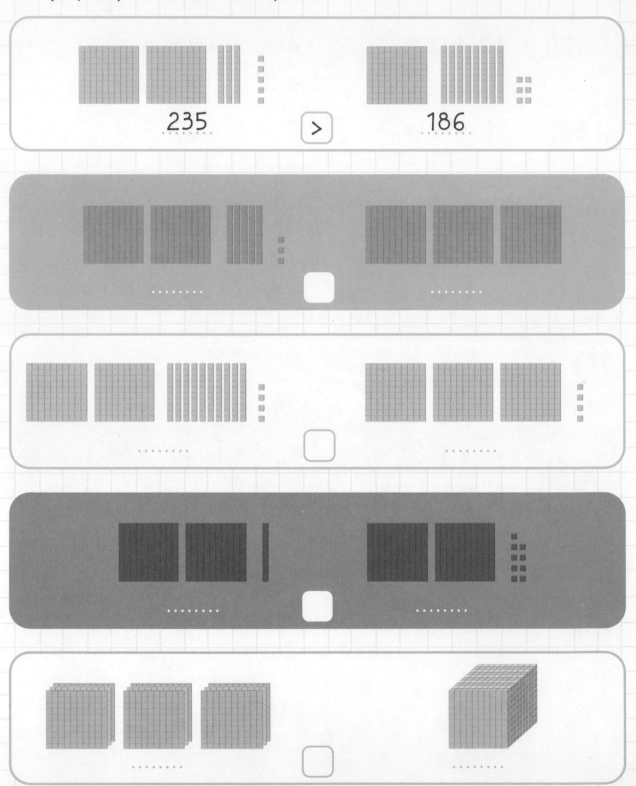

235 **>** 186

Compare Numbers

1 Write < (less than), > (greater than), or = (equals) between each pair.

397 **<** 401

734 ☐ 734

899 ☐ 200

333 ☐ 422

1000 ☐ 999

604 ☐ 587

554 ☐ 545

1000 ☐ 1000

654 ☐ 456

659 ☐ 660

529 ☐ 531

799 ☐ 898

909 ☐ 910

853 ☐ 853

100 ☐ 1000

2 Write another number to complete each number sentence.

200 > ....   524 = ...   999 < ....

824 = ...   303 < ....   299 > ....

Smallest to Largest

Write the numbers in order from smallest to largest.

| 48 | 1000 | 692 | 3 | 989 | 177 | 823 | 425 |

| 923 | 1 | 855 | 523 | 999 | 231 | 86 | 683 |

| 723 | 396 | 28 | 8 | 1000 | 101 | 376 | 834 |

| 499 | 501 | 393 | 11 | 835 | 1000 | 42 | 888 |

| 82 | 734 | 733 | 83 | 921 | 202 | 2 | 210 |

| 562 | 832 | 90 | 124 | 6 | 1000 | 462 | 0 |

The Ant Challenge

There are more than 1000 ants on this page.
Follow the steps to circle exactly 1000 of them.

1 Circle 10 groups of 10. This is 100 ants.
2 Do this 10 times. You have now circled 1000 ants.

How many ants are there on this page altogether? [ ]

Addition to 10

Knowing the 1-digit addition facts by heart makes math easier.
Time how long it takes you to solve these problems.
Another day, cover the answers and try to beat your time.

5 + 4 = ☐   3 + 6 = ☐   9 + 1 = ☐

1 + 7 = ☐   2 + 3 = ☐   4 + 2 = ☐

8 + 2 = ☐   3 + 5 = ☐   2 + 6 = ☐

4 + 3 = ☐   5 + 2 = ☐   7 + 2 = ☐

9 + 1 = ☐   7 + 1 = ☐   4 + 4 = ☐

6 + 2 = ☐   3 + 3 = ☐   2 + 5 = ☐

2 + 2 = ☐   5 + 3 = ☐   3 + 4 = ☐

7 + 3 = ☐   5 + 5 = ☐   1 + 8 = ☐

The first time I did this, my time was ....

The second time I did this, my time was ....

Addition to 20

Solve the word problems and show your work in the box.

Lucy had 4 toy cars. Then her brother gave her 6 more. How many cars did she have now?

Lucas counted 12 ducklings. Then 3 more hatched. How many ducklings were there now?

Riley had 7 neighbors. Then 5 more moved in. How many neighbors did she have now?

Max polished 14 shoes. Then he polished 6 more. How many did he polish altogether?

Eve learned 8 songs. Then she learned the same number again. How many did she learn altogether?

Dylan had 13 model dinosaurs. Then he was given 7 more. How many did he have now?

Odd or Even?

Circle pairs of objects to figure out if there is an odd or even number. Check odd or even.

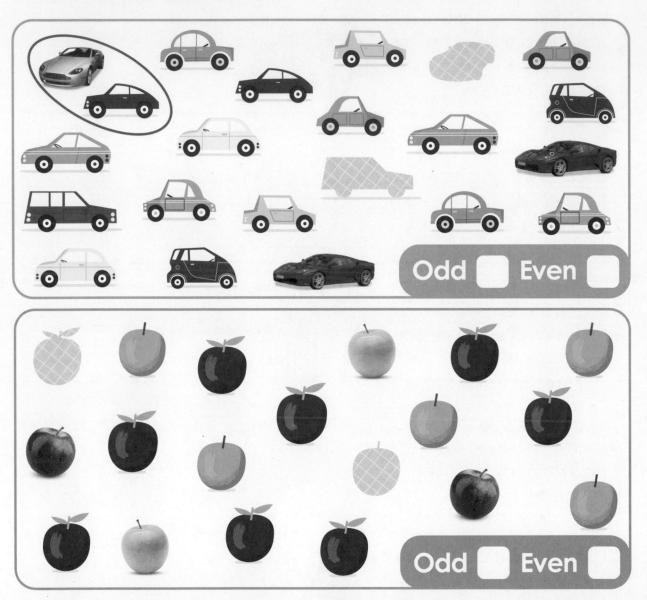

Odd ☐ Even ☐

Odd ☐ Even ☐

Even numbers end in 0, 2, 4, 6, or 8. Odd numbers end in 1, 3, 5, 7, or 9. Shade the **odd** numbers **orange** and the **even** numbers **blue**.

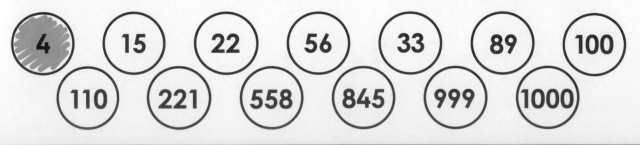

4 15 22 56 33 89 100

110 221 558 845 999 1000

Share It Evenly

Use your doubles knowledge to solve the problems. For each problem, the numbers in all the boxes should be the same.

Tom shares 10 toy cars evenly with his sister. How many do they get each? ☐

10 = ☐ + ☐

Ella shares 14 books evenly with her friend. How many do they get each? ☐

14 = ☐ + ☐

Joe shares 18 apples evenly with his dad. How many do they get each? ☐

18 = ☐ + ☐

Lily shares 20 candies evenly with her brother. How many do they get each? ☐

20 = ☐ + ☐

Luke shares 100 marbles evenly with his friend. How many do they get each? ☐

100 = ☐ + ☐

Write **T** for true or **F** for false.

When two people share things evenly, each person gets the same amount. ☐

When two people share things evenly, one person gets more than the other. ☐

When two people share things evenly, they get half each. ☐

Make 10

Fill in the missing numbers. What patterns can you see?

0 + ☐ = 10	and	☐ + 0 = 10
1 + ☐ = 10	and	☐ + 1 = 10
2 + ☐ = 10	and	☐ + 2 = 10
3 + ☐ = 10	and	☐ + 3 = 10
4 + ☐ = 10	and	☐ + 4 = 10
5 + ☐ = 10	and	☐ + 5 = 10
6 + ☐ = 10	and	☐ + 6 = 10
7 + ☐ = 10	and	☐ + 7 = 10
8 + ☐ = 10	and	☐ + 8 = 10
9 + ☐ = 10	and	☐ + 9 = 10

To solve each problem, circle two numbers that add up to 10, and then add the remaining number to 10.

⑦ + 5 + ③ = 10 + 5 = 15

6 + 4 + 7 = 10 + ☐ = ☐

5 + 2 + 8 = 10 + ☐ = ☐

1 + 4 + 9 = 10 + ☐ = ☐

9 + 5 + 5 = 10 + ☐ = ☐

4 + 6 + 4 = 10 + ☐ = ☐

Break the second number into two to help you make 10
and solve the problems.

4 + 7 = 4 + ⬚6 + ⬚1 = 10 + ⬚1 = ⬚11

3 + 9 = 3 + ⬚ + ⬚ = 10 + ⬚ = ⬚

6 + 8 = 6 + ⬚ + ⬚ = 10 + ⬚ = ⬚

5 + 6 = 5 + ⬚ + ⬚ = 10 + ⬚ = ⬚

8 + 9 = 8 + ⬚ + ⬚ = 10 + ⬚ = ⬚

7 + 6 = 7 + ⬚ + ⬚ = 10 + ⬚ = ⬚

Draw lines linking the numbers that add up to 10
to help you solve the problems.

4 + 7 + 3 + 6 + 2 = 10 + 10 + ⬚2 = ⬚22

5 + 6 + 1 + 4 + 5 = 10 + 10 + ⬚ = ⬚

6 + 1 + 9 + 3 + 7 = 10 + 10 + ⬚ = ⬚

2 + 7 + 8 + 4 + 3 = 10 + 10 + ⬚ = ⬚

3 + 5 + 5 + 0 + 7 = 10 + 10 + ⬚ = ⬚

5 + 5 + 5 + 8 + 5 = 10 + 10 + ⬚ = ⬚

Borrow to Make 10

If a number is just below 10, we can borrow from the other number to make it up to 10. Use this strategy to solve the problems. Draw arrows to show what you are moving.

9 + 4 ★ ★ ★ ★ ★ ★ ★ ★ ★ ★ ★ ★ ★

I take [1] from 4 and give it to the 9.   9 + 4 = 10 + [3] = [13]

9 + 7 ♥ ♥ ♥ ♥ ♥ ♥ ♥ ♥   ♥ ♥ ♥ ♥ ♥ ♥ ♥

I take [ ] from 7 and give it to the 9.   9 + 7 = 10 + [ ] = [ ]

9 + 5 🔘 🔘 🔘 🔘 🔘 🔘 🔘 🔘 🔘   🔘 🔘 🔘 🔘 🔘

I take [ ] from 5 and give it to the 9.   9 + 5 = 10 + [ ] = [ ]

8 + 4 😊 😊 😊 😊 😊 😊 😊 😊   😊 😊 😊 😊

I take [ ] from 4 and give it to the 8.   8 + 4 = 10 + [ ] = [ ]

9 + 2 🐱 🐱 🐱 🐱 🐱 🐱 🐱 🐱 🐱   🐱 🐱

I take [ ] from [ ] and give it to the 9.   9 + 2 = 10 + [ ] = [ ]

8 + 6 🐶 🐶 🐶 🐶 🐶 🐶 🐶 🐶   🐶 🐶 🐶 🐶 🐶 🐶

I take [ ] from [ ] and give it to the 8.   8 + 6 = 10 + [ ] = [ ]

Jump Strategy

Use number lines to solve these problems. Jump in tens and then in ones. The first one is done for you.

45 + 32 = **45 +** 30 + 2 = 77

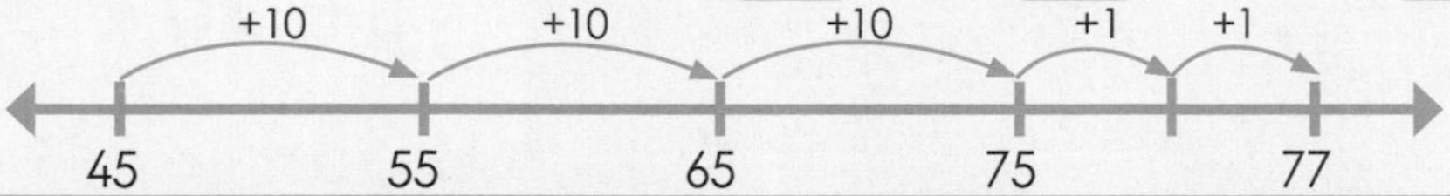

+10 +10 +10 +1 +1

45 55 65 75 77

37 + 21 = **37 +** ☐ + ☐ = ☐

37

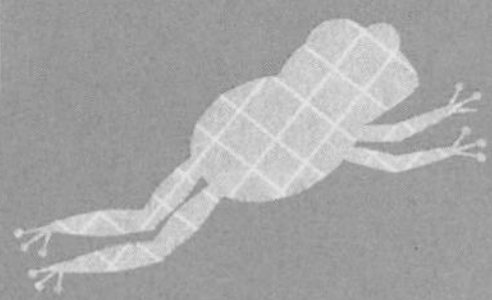

63 + 23 = **63 +** ☐ + ☐ = ☐

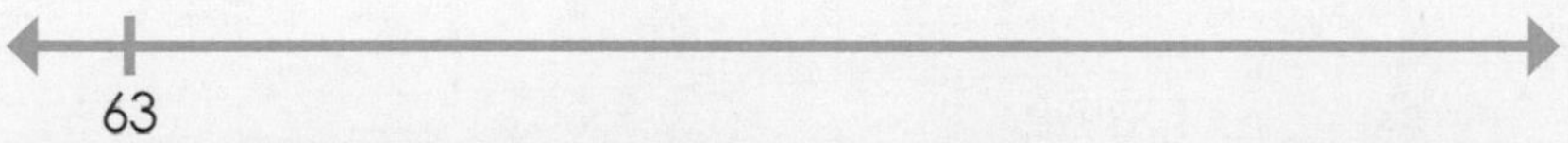

63

58 + 33 = **58 +** ☐ + ☐ = ☐

58

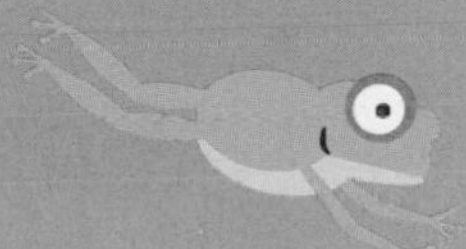

75 + 24 = **75 +** ☐ + ☐ = ☐

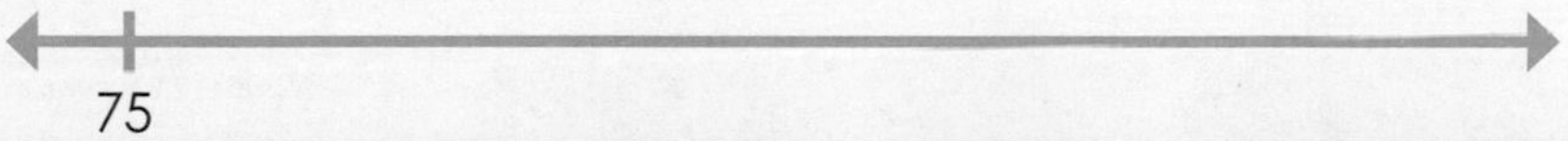

75

49 + 34 = **49 +** ☐ + ☐ = ☐

49

85 + 15 = **85 +** ☐ + ☐ = ☐

85

Number Line Jumps

Jump up the number line from the first number to the answer.
Where you can, jump in tens. Then add up your jumps.

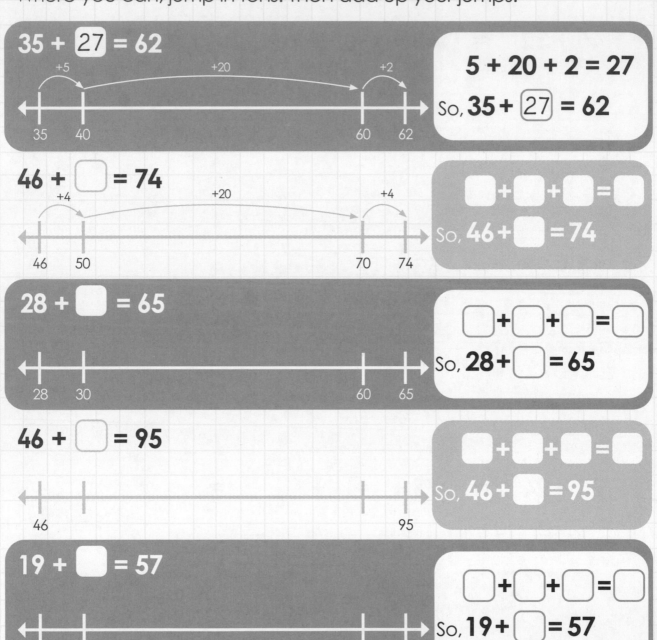

35 + 27 = 62

+5   +20   +2

35 40   60 62

5 + 20 + 2 = 27

So, **35 + 27 = 62**

46 + ☐ = 74

+4   +20   +4

46 50   70 74

☐ + ☐ + ☐ = ☐

So, **46 + ☐ = 74**

28 + ☐ = 65

28 30   60 65

☐ + ☐ + ☐ = ☐

So, **28 + ☐ = 65**

46 + ☐ = 95

46   95

☐ + ☐ + ☐ = ☐

So, **46 + ☐ = 95**

19 + ☐ = 57

☐ + ☐ + ☐ = ☐

So, **19 + ☐ = 57**

65 + ☐ = 94

☐ + ☐ + ☐ = ☐

So, **65 + ☐ = 94**

Adding 1's and 10's

Break the two-digit number into tens and ones to help solve the problems.

$12 + 4$ = $10 + \boxed{2} + 4$ = $10 + \boxed{6}$ = $\boxed{16}$

$15 + 3$ = $10 + \boxed{} + 3$ = $10 + \boxed{}$ = $\boxed{}$

$11 + 6$ = $10 + \boxed{} + 6$ = $10 + \boxed{}$ = $\boxed{}$

$16 + 2$ = $10 + \boxed{} + 2$ = $10 + \boxed{}$ = $\boxed{}$

$24 + 4$ = $20 + \boxed{} + 4$ = $20 + \boxed{}$ = $\boxed{}$

$57 + 2$ = $50 + \boxed{} + 2$ = $50 + \boxed{}$ = $\boxed{}$

$32 + 7$ = $30 + \boxed{} + 7$ = $30 + \boxed{}$ = $\boxed{}$

$63 + 5$ = $60 + \boxed{} + 5$ = $60 + \boxed{}$ = $\boxed{}$

$91 + 8$ = $90 + \boxed{} + 8$ = $90 + \boxed{}$ = $\boxed{}$

$55 + 5$ = $50 + \boxed{} + 5$ = $50 + \boxed{}$ = $\boxed{}$

Place-Value Partitioning

Break the numbers into tens and ones to help solve the problems.

34 + 52 = (30 + 50) + (4 + 2) = 80 + 6 = 86
tens   ones

27 + 41 = (20 + 40) + (7 + 1) = ☐ + ☐ = ☐
tens   ones

65 + 34 = (60 + 30) + (5 + 4) = ☐ + ☐ = ☐
tens   ones

72 + 26 = (70 + 20) + (2 + 6) = ☐ + ☐ = ☐
tens   ones

45 + 23 = (☐ + ☐) + (☐ + ☐) = ☐ + ☐ = ☐
tens   ones

18 + 71 = (☐ + ☐) + (☐ + ☐) = ☐ + ☐ = ☐
tens   ones

56 + 43 = (☐ + ☐) + (☐ + ☐) = ☐ + ☐ = ☐
tens   ones

88 + 11 = (☐ + ☐) + (☐ + ☐) = ☐ + ☐ = ☐
tens   ones

71 + 27 = (☐ + ☐) + (☐ + ☐) = ☐ + ☐ = ☐
tens   ones

35 + 62 = (☐ + ☐) + (☐ + ☐) = ☐ + ☐ = ☐
tens   ones

Place-Value Partitioning

Break the numbers into hundreds, tens, and ones to help solve the problems.

427 + 362 = (400 + 300) + (20 + 60) + (7 + 2) = $\boxed{700}$ + $\boxed{80}$ + $\boxed{9}$ = $\boxed{789}$

215 + 573 = (200 + 500) + (10 + 70) + (5 + 3) = ☐ + ☐ + ☐ = ☐

725 + 152 = (700 + 100) + (20 + 50) + (5 + 2) = ☐ + ☐ + ☐ = ☐

362 + 335 = (300 + 300) + (60 + 30) + (2 + 5) = ☐ + ☐ + ☐ = ☐

624 + 241 = (☐ + ☐) + (☐ + ☐) + (☐ + ☐) = ☐ + ☐ + ☐ = ☐

537 + 432 = (☐ + ☐) + (☐ + ☐) + (☐ + ☐) = ☐ + ☐ + ☐ = ☐

123 + 321 = (☐ + ☐) + (☐ + ☐) + (☐ + ☐) = ☐ + ☐ + ☐ = ☐

777 + 212 = (☐ + ☐) + (☐ + ☐) + (☐ + ☐) = ☐ + ☐ + ☐ = ☐

544 + 242 = (☐ + ☐) + (☐ + ☐) + (☐ + ☐) = ☐ + ☐ + ☐ = ☐

811 + 188 = (☐ + ☐) + (☐ + ☐) + (☐ + ☐) = ☐ + ☐ + ☐ = ☐

Adding in Columns

We can add tens and ones in columns. Add the numbers in the ones column first. Then add the numbers in the tens column.

	Tens	Ones
	3	4
+	5	1
	8	5

	Tens	Ones
	6	2
+	3	4

	Tens	Ones
	4	7
+	2	1

	Tens	Ones
	1	6
+	6	1

34 + 51 = 85

62 + 34 =

47 + 21 =

16 + 61 =

Now add 3-digit numbers in columns. Add the ones column first. Then add the tens column, and finally add the hundreds column.

	Hundreds	Tens	Ones
	5	2	3
+	1	0	4
	6	2	7

	Hundreds	Tens	Ones
	2	7	1
+	4	2	6

523 + 104 = 627

271 + 426 =

	Hundreds	Tens	Ones
	3	4	2
+	3	5	0

	Hundreds	Tens	Ones
	6	7	1
+	1	0	6

342 + 350 =

671 + 106 =

Adding in Columns

Add the ones and tens columns to solve the problems.

42	72	55	86
+ 36	+ 25	+ 44	+ 13
78			

34	12	81	24
+ 62	+ 46	+ 18	+ 41

Add the ones, tens, and hundreds columns to solve the problems.

426	213	625	413
+ 203	+ 452	+ 374	+ 330
629			

502	420
+ 222	+ 422

600	713
+ 235	+ 804

Borrow to Make 100

If a number is just below 100, we can borrow from the other number to make it up to 100. Use this strategy to solve the problems.

98 + 14

I take ⟦2⟧ from 14 and give it to 98.

98 + 14 = 100 + ⟦12⟧ = ⟦112⟧

99 + 25

I take ⟦1⟧ from 25 and give it to 99.

99 + 25 = 100 + ⟦ ⟧ = ⟦ ⟧

98 + 42

I take ⟦ ⟧ from 42 and give it to 98.

98 + 42 = 100 + ⟦ ⟧ = ⟦ ⟧

97 + 33

I take ⟦ ⟧ from 33 and give it to 97.

97 + 33 = 100 + ⟦ ⟧ = ⟦ ⟧

Now try the same thing with numbers near other hundreds.

199 + 23

I take ⟦ ⟧ from 23 and give it to 199.

199 + 23 = 200 + ⟦ ⟧ = ⟦ ⟧

298 + 47

I take ⟦ ⟧ from 47 and give it to 298.

298 + 47 = 300 + ⟦ ⟧ = ⟦ ⟧

397 + 54

I take ⟦ ⟧ from 54 and give it to 397.

394 + 54 = ⟦ ⟧ + ⟦ ⟧ = ⟦ ⟧

598 + 31

I take ⟦ ⟧ from 31 and give it to 598.

598 + 31 = ⟦ ⟧ + ⟦ ⟧ = ⟦ ⟧

Rounding Up

You can round up a number to a ten (10, 20, 30, etc.) to make addition easier. You must then take away the extra number you added. Solve these problems using this strategy.

35 + 28 = (35 + 30) – [2] = [65] – 2 = [63]

56 + 39 = (56 + 40) – [ ] = [ ] – 1 = [ ]

42 + 19 = (42 + 20) – [ ] = [ ] – 1 = [ ]

66 + 28 = (66 + 30) – [ ] = [ ] – 2 = [ ]

14 + 59 = (14 + 60) – [ ] = [ ] – [ ] = [ ]

25 + 48 = (25 + 50) – [ ] = [ ] – [ ] = [ ]

74 + 18 = (74 + [ ]) – [ ] = [ ] – [ ] = [ ]

33 + 58 = (33 + [ ]) – [ ] = [ ] – [ ] = [ ]

Rounding Up

You can round up a number to a hundred (100, 200, 300, etc.) to make addition easier. You must then take away the extra number you added. Solve these problems using this strategy.

43 + 197 = (43 + 200) – 3 = 243 – 3 = 240

36 + 198 = (36 + 200) – ☐ = ☐ – 2 = ☐

55 + 299 = (55 + 300) – ☐ = ☐ – 1 = ☐

47 + 297 = (47 + 300) – ☐ = ☐ – 3 = ☐

65 + 398 = (65 + 400) – ☐ = ☐ – ☐ = ☐

74 + 599 = (74 + 600) – ☐ = ☐ – ☐ = ☐

46 + 498 = (46 + ☐) – ☐ = ☐ – ☐ = ☐

53 + 897 = (53 + ☐) – ☐ = ☐ – ☐ = ☐

Two-Digit Addition

Add the ones and then the tens to help solve these problems.

	Tens	Ones
	2	8
+	4	5
	7	3

	Tens	Ones
	3	6
+	2	5

	Tens	Ones
	5	7
+	1	8

8 + 5 = 13
20 + 40 = 60
13 + 60 = 73

6 + 5 = ☐
30 + 20 = ☐
☐ + ☐ = ☐

7 + 8 = ☐
50 + 10 = ☐
☐ + ☐ = ☐

Solve the problems to practice two-digit addition with regrouping.

$\overset{1}{6}5$
+ 6
71

34
+ 8

48
+ 25

25
+ 27

68
+ 16

39
+ 33

57
+ 34

53
+ 48

Three-Digit Addition

Solve the problems to practice three-digit addition using regrouping.

```
 1 1
 125          148          273          192
+ 87         + 74         + 49        + 129
─────        ─────        ─────       ─────
 212
```

```
 364          266          444          635
+136         +266         +457         +305
─────        ─────        ─────        ─────
```

```
 328          548          720          499
+274         +188         +280         +501
─────        ─────        ─────        ─────
```

Word Problems

Solve the word problems and show your work in the box.

Tom had 3 books, Mila had 6, Jack had 7, and Luna had 4. How many books did they have altogether?

There were 45 boys and 53 girls learning to swim. How many children were learning to swim altogether?

There were 36 girls learning judo and 37 boys. How many children were learning judo altogether?

A shop had 63 customers. Then 5 more arrived. How many customers did it have now?

A ferryboat had 45 passengers. Then 23 more passengers boarded. How many passengers were in the boat now?

On Saturday, 357 children saw a movie. On Sunday, 265 children saw the same movie. How many children saw the movie over the weekend?

Describe Arrays

Fill in the gaps to describe the arrays.

There are ____ rows. Each row has ____ dots.
There are ____ columns. Each column has ____ dots.
Altogether, there are ____ dots.

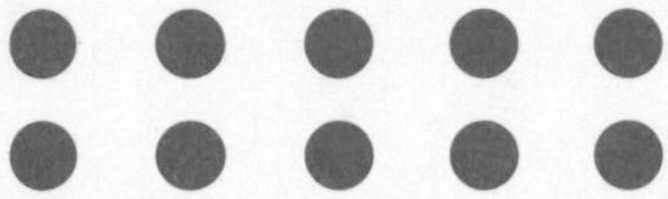

There are ____ rows. Each row has ____ dots.
There are ____ columns. Each column has ____ dots.
Altogether, there are ____ dots.

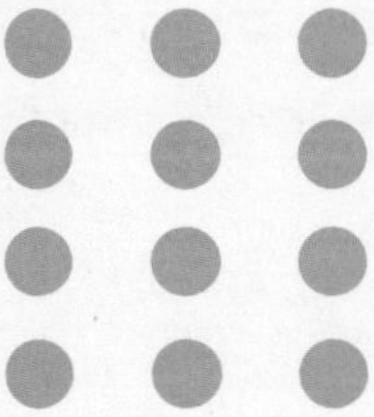

There are ____ rows. Each row has ____ dots.
There are ____ columns. Each column has ____ dots.
Altogether, there are ____ dots.

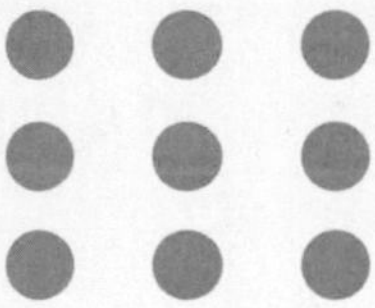

There are ____ rows. Each row has ____ dots.
There are ____ columns. Each column has ____ dots.
Altogether, there are ____ dots.

Fill in the gaps to describe the arrays.

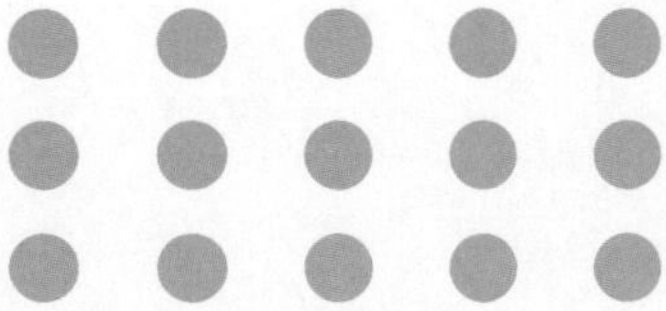

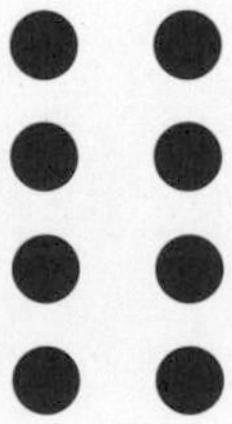

$5 + 5 + 5 =$ ☐

$2 + 2 + 2 + 2 =$ ☐

$3 + 3 + 3 + 3 + 3 =$ ☐

$4 + 4 =$ ☐

Make Arrays

Circle groups of 4. Then draw the groups of 4 as rows in the grid.

 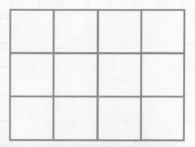

Add in rows: 4 + 4 + 4 = ☐

Adding columns: 3 + 3 + 3 + 3 = ☐

Circle groups of 5. Then draw the groups of 5 as rows in the grid.

Add in rows: ☐ + ☐ = ☐

Adding columns: ☐ + ☐ + ☐ + ☐ + ☐ = ☐

Circle groups of 6. Then draw the groups of 6 as rows in the grid.

Add in rows: ☐ + ☐ + ☐ = ☐

Adding columns: ☐ + ☐ + ☐ + ☐ + ☐ + ☐ = ☐

Focus on 5 and 6

Color the cubes to show the problems. Then write the answers.

5 − 2 = ☐
5 − 3 = ☐

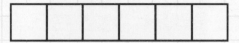

5 − 4 = ☐
5 − 1 = ☐

6 − 4 = ☐
6 − 2 = ☐

6 − 3 = ☐
6 − ☐ = 3

Write the missing number in each number triangle.

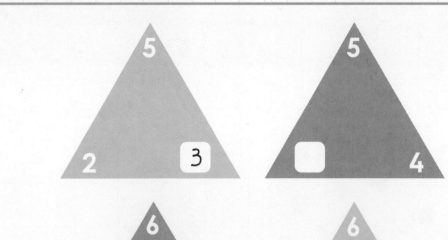

Focus on 7 and 8

Color the cubes to show the problems. Then write the answers.

$7 - 3 =$ ☐
$7 - 4 =$ ☐

$7 - 5 =$ ☐
$7 - 2 =$ ☐

$8 - 3 =$ ☐
$8 - 5 =$ ☐

$8 - 2 =$ ☐
$8 - 6 =$ ☐

Write the missing number in each number triangle.

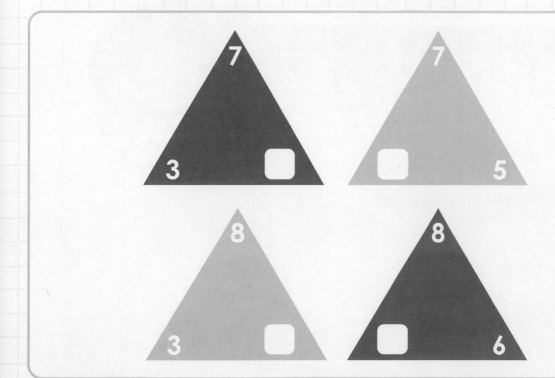

Focus on 9

Color the cubes to show the problems. Then write the answers.

9 − 4 = ☐
9 − 5 = ☐

9 − 3 = ☐
9 − 6 = ☐

9 − 7 = ☐
9 − 2 = ☐

9 − 8 = ☐
9 − 1 = ☐

Fill in the numbers to make a subtraction table. Subtract the numbers down the side from the numbers along the top.

−	10	9	8	7	6	5	4	3	2	1
1	9	8	7	6	5	4	3	2	1	0
2						3				
3			5							
4	6									
5					1					
6										
7		2								
8										
9										
10	0									

Subtraction Below 10

Knowing the 1-digit subtraction facts by heart makes math easier. Time how long it takes to solve these problems. On another day, cover the answers and try to beat your time.

8 – 4 = ☐   3 – 1 = ☐   9 – 6 = ☐

7 – 3 = ☐   5 – 2 = ☐   6 – 3 = ☐

2 – 1 = ☐   10 – 7 = ☐   4 – 2 = ☐

4 – 3 = ☐   5 – 3 = ☐   7 – 2 = ☐

9 – 5 = ☐   7 – 5 = ☐   4 – 1 = ☐

6 – 4 = ☐   3 – 2 = ☐   2 – 2 = ☐

8 – 2 = ☐   9 – 7 = ☐   5 – 4 = ☐

7 – 4 = ☐   6 – 2 = ☐   8 – 3 = ☐

The first time I did this, my time was.......................................

The second time I did this, my time was............................

Subtraction Below 20

Solve the word problems and show your work in the box.

Mason had 15 pet mice. Then he sold 10 to a pet shop. How many mice did he have left?

Bella baked 20 cupcakes. Then her friends ate 7 of them. How many cupcakes were left?

Matt had 12 comics. His baby brother ripped up 6 of them. How many did he have left?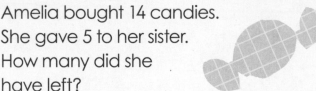

Amelia bought 14 candies. She gave 5 to her sister. How many did she have left?

Jacob baked 16 cookies. He dropped 8 of them. How many cookies did he have left?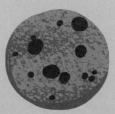

Mia had 8 T-shirts. She outgrew half of them. How many T-shirts still fitted her?

Focus **on** 10

Fill in the missing numbers. What patterns can you see?

10 – ☐ = 10   and   10 – ☐ = 0
10 – ☐ = 9   and   10 – ☐ = 1
10 – ☐ = 8   and   10 – ☐ = 2
10 – ☐ = 7   and   10 – ☐ = 3
10 – ☐ = 6   and   10 – ☐ = 4
10 – ☐ = 5   and   10 – ☐ = 5
10 – ☐ = 4   and   10 – ☐ = 6
10 – ☐ = 3   and   10 – ☐ = 7
10 – ☐ = 2   and   10 – ☐ = 8
10 – ☐ = 1   and   10 – ☐ = 9

Fill in the missing numbers.

18 – 8 = ☐   13 – ☐ = 10   20 – 10 = ☐

☐ – 7 = 10   19 – 9 = ☐   16 – ☐ = 10

11 – 1 = ☐   ☐ – 5 = 10   12 – 2 = ☐

14 – ☐ = 10   10 – 0 = ☐   ☐ – 10 = 10

Subtract to 10

Circle the two numbers that subtract to 10 to help you solve each problem.

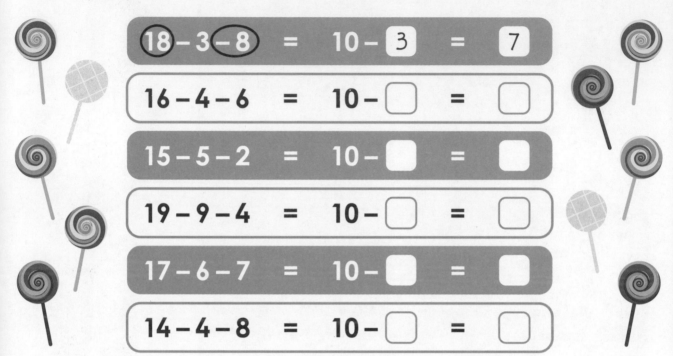

(18) − 3 − (8) = 10 − [3] = [7]

16 − 4 − 6 = 10 − ☐ = ☐

15 − 5 − 2 = 10 − ☐ = ☐

19 − 9 − 4 = 10 − ☐ = ☐

17 − 6 − 7 = 10 − ☐ = ☐

14 − 4 − 8 = 10 − ☐ = ☐

Circle the two numbers that subtract to 20 to help you solve each problem.

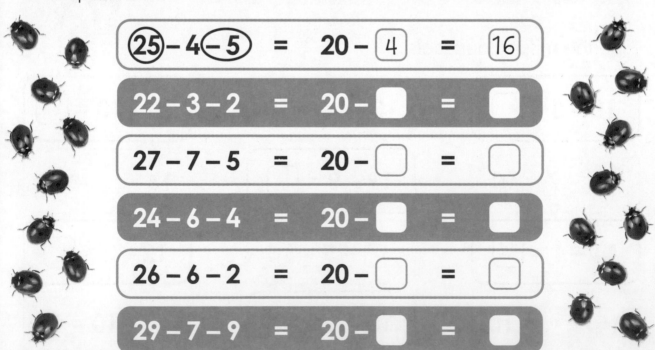

(25) − 4 − (5) = 20 − [4] = [16]

22 − 3 − 2 = 20 − ☐ = ☐

27 − 7 − 5 = 20 − ☐ = ☐

24 − 6 − 4 = 20 − ☐ = ☐

26 − 6 − 2 = 20 − ☐ = ☐

29 − 7 − 9 = 20 − ☐ = ☐

Subtract a Ten

Use the hundred chart to help you subtract multiples of 10.

1	2	3	4	5	6	7	8	9	10
11	12	13	14	15	16	17	18	19	20
21	22	23	24	25	26	27	28	29	30
31	32	33	34	35	36	37	38	39	40
41	42	43	44	45	46	47	48	49	50
51	52	53	54	55	56	57	58	59	60
61	62	63	64	65	66	67	68	69	70
71	72	73	74	75	76	77	78	79	80
81	82	83	84	85	86	87	88	89	90
91	92	93	94	95	96	97	98	99	100

37 – 20 = ☐   54 – 10 = ☐   78 – 20 = ☐

63 – 30 = ☐   72 – 40 = ☐   90 – 30 = ☐

86 – ☐ = 56   50 – ☐ = 20   34 – ☐ = 24

☐ – 20 = 42   ☐ – 40 = 28   ☐ – 30 = 70

Make 10 to Subtract

To figure out 14 − 5 = ?, you can flip the problem and use addition. Use this strategy to solve these problems. Jump up the number line, and then add up the jumps.

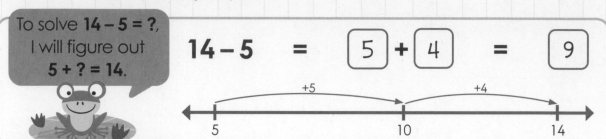

To solve **14 − 5 = ?**, I will figure out **5 + ? = 14.**

14 − 5 = 5 + 4 = 9

+5   +4
5   10   14

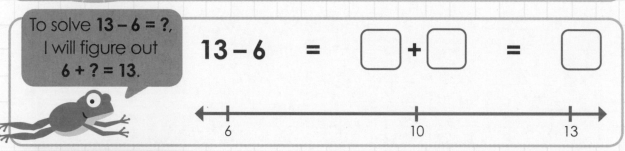

To solve **13 − 6 = ?**, I will figure out **6 + ? = 13.**

13 − 6 = ☐ + ☐ = ☐

6   10   13

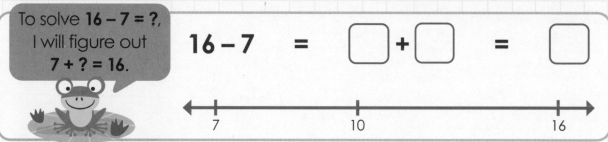

To solve **16 − 7 = ?**, I will figure out **7 + ? = 16.**

16 − 7 = ☐ + ☐ = ☐

7   10   16

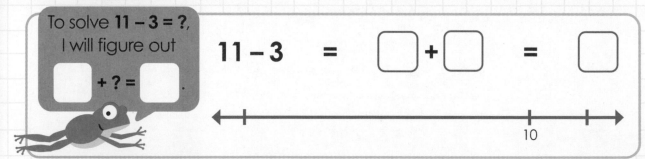

To solve **11 − 3 = ?**, I will figure out ☐ + ? = ☐ .

11 − 3 = ☐ + ☐ = ☐

10

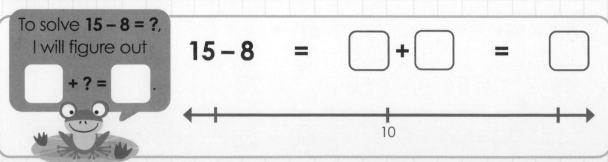

To solve **15 − 8 = ?**, I will figure out ☐ + ? = ☐ .

15 − 8 = ☐ + ☐ = ☐

10

170

Make Tens to Subtract

You can use the strategy on the opposite page to solve problems with larger numbers. Jump in multiples of 10 where you can. Use this strategy to solve the problems on the number lines.

To solve **53 – 26 = ?**, I will figure out **26 + ? = 53**.

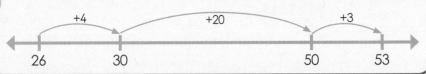

53 – 26 = $\boxed{4}$ + $\boxed{20}$ + $\boxed{3}$ = $\boxed{27}$

+4   +20   +3

26   30   50   53

To solve **74 – 35 = ?**, I will figure out **35 + ? = 74**.

74 – 35 = $\boxed{}$ + $\boxed{}$ + $\boxed{}$ = $\boxed{}$

35   40   70   74

To solve **41 – 27 = ?**, I will figure out **27 + ? = 41**.

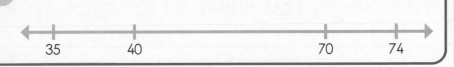

41 – 27 = $\boxed{}$ + $\boxed{}$ + $\boxed{}$ = $\boxed{}$

27   30   40   41

To solve **55 – 28 = ?**, I will figure out $\boxed{}$ **+ ? =** $\boxed{}$.

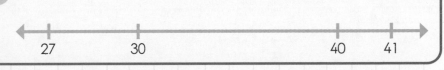

55 – 28 = $\boxed{}$ + $\boxed{}$ + $\boxed{}$ = $\boxed{}$

To solve **82 – 46 = ?**, I will figure out $\boxed{}$ **+ ? =** $\boxed{}$.

82 – 46 = $\boxed{}$ + $\boxed{}$ + $\boxed{}$ = $\boxed{}$

Place-Value Partitioning

Break the numbers into tens and ones to help solve the problems.

67 − 43 = (60 − 40) + (7 − 3) = ⟨20⟩ + ⟨4⟩ = ⟨24⟩
                  tens   ones

83 − 62 = (80 − 60) + (3 − 2) = ☐ + ☐ = ☐
                  tens   ones

59 − 37 = (50 − 30) + (9 − 7) = ☐ + ☐ = ☐
                  tens   ones

66 − 55 = (60 − 50) + (6 − 5) = ☐ + ☐ = ☐
                  tens   ones

47 − 31 = (☐ − ☐) + (☐ − ☐) = ☐ + ☐ = ☐
                  tens   ones

99 − 35 = (☐ − ☐) + (☐ − ☐) = ☐ + ☐ = ☐
                  tens   ones

36 − 16 = (☐ − ☐) + (☐ − ☐) = ☐ + ☐ = ☐
                  tens   ones

61 − 40 = (☐ − ☐) + (☐ − ☐) = ☐ + ☐ = ☐
                  tens   ones

45 − 42 = (☐ − ☐) + (☐ − ☐) = ☐ + ☐ = ☐
                  tens   ones

97 − 87 = (☐ − ☐) + (☐ − ☐) = ☐ + ☐ = ☐
                  tens   ones

Subtract in Columns

We can subtract tens and ones in columns. Subtract the numbers in the ones column first. Then subtract the numbers in the tens column.

	Tens	Ones
	6	4
–	4	3
=	2	1

	Tens	Ones
	7	6
–	5	2
=		

	Tens	Ones
	8	3
–	4	0
=		

Now subtract 3-digit numbers in columns. Subtract the ones column first. Then subtract the tens column, and finally subtract the hundreds column.

	Hundreds	Tens	Ones
	7	4	5
–	6	2	4
=	1	2	1

	Hundreds	Tens	Ones
	6	3	8
–	4	2	5
=			

	Hundreds	Tens	Ones
	5	9	4
–	3	7	0
=			

	Hundreds	Tens	Ones
	4	6	7
–	1	0	6
=			

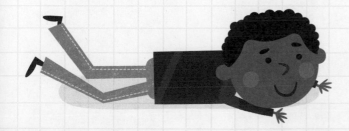

Subtract in Columns

Subtract the ones and tens columns to solve the problems.

84	96	75	38
− 53	− 35	− 41	− 16
= 31	= ☐	= ☐	= ☐

55	96	61	99
− 33	− 63	− 40	− 82
= ☐	= ☐	= ☐	= ☐

Subtract the ones, tens, and hundreds columns to solve the problems.

859	756	958
− 427	− 535	− 327
= 432	= ☐	= ☐

635	538	945
− 425	− 215	− 830
= ☐	= ☐	= ☐

444	773	362
− 210	− 632	− 351
= ☐	= ☐	= ☐

Compensation

You can increase the number you're taking away to a multiple of ten (20, 30, 40, etc.) to make subtraction easier. Then add back the extra number you took away. Use this strategy and draw number lines to solve these problems.

$65 - 18 = (65 - 20) + 2 = 45 + 2 = 47$

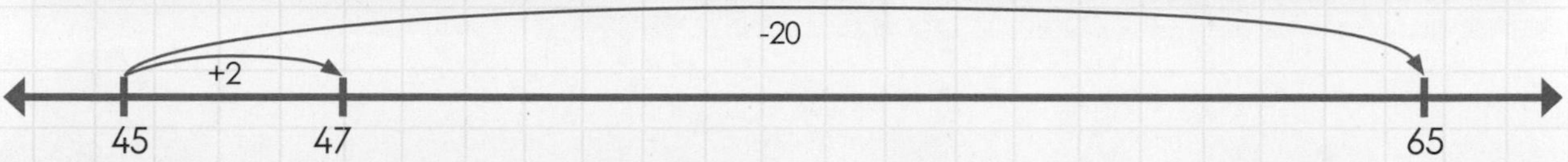

-20 +2
45 47 65

$54 - 19 = (54 - 20) + \square = \square + \square = \square$

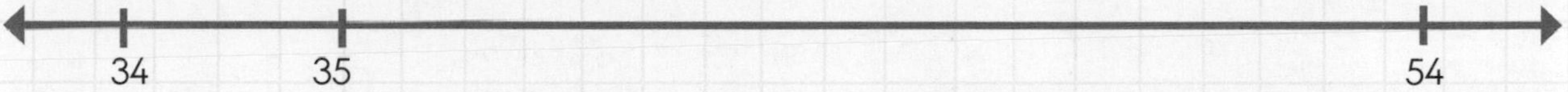

34 35 54

$36 - 28 = (36 - 30) + \square = \square + \square = \square$

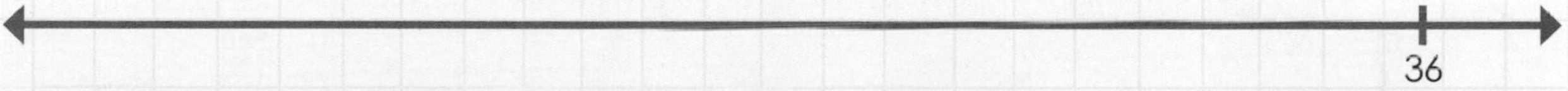

36

$47 - 29 = (47 - \square) + \square = \square + \square = \square$

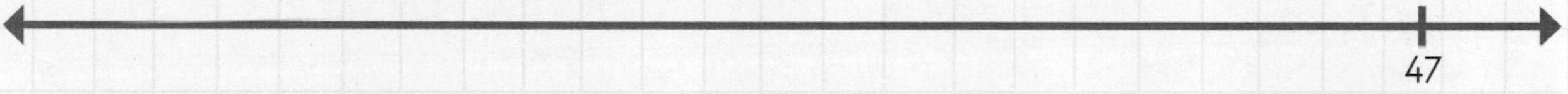

47

$55 - 37 = (55 - \square) + \square = \square + \square = \square$

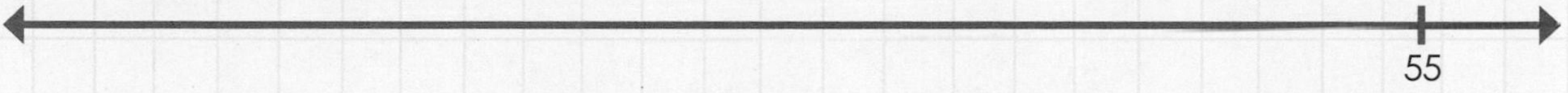

55

$93 - 48 = (93 - \square) + \square = \square + \square = \square$

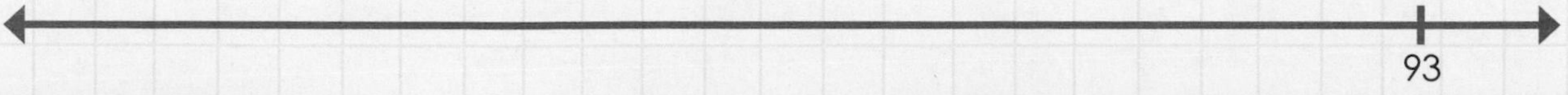

93

Shifting Up

If you add the same number to both sides of a subtraction problem, the difference is still the same. Use this strategy to make the problems easier.

42 − 19   I will add [1] to both sides of the problem.

42 − 19 = [43] − [20] = [23]

65 − 29   I will add [ ] to both sides of the problem.

65 − 29 = [ ] − [ ] = [ ]

74 − 18   I will add [ ] to both sides of the problem.

74 − 18 = [ ] − [ ] = [ ]

56 − 39   I will add [ ] to both sides of the problem.

56 − 39 = [ ] − [ ] = [ ]

45 − 17   I will add [ ] to both sides of the problem.

45 − 17 = [ ] − [ ] = [ ]

73 − 48   I will add [ ] to both sides of the problem.

73 − 48 = [ ] − [ ] = [ ]

92 − 27   I will add [ ] to both sides of the problem.

92 − 27 = [ ] − [ ] = [ ]

Shifting Down

If you subtract the same number from both sides of a subtraction problem, the difference is still the same. Use this strategy to make the problems easier.

77 – 23   I will subtract **3** from both sides of the problem.

77 – 23 = **74** – **20** = **54**

55 – 32   I will subtract ☐ from both sides of the problem.

55 – 32 = ☐ – ☐ = ☐

88 – 54   I will subtract ☐ from both sides of the problem.

88 – 54 = ☐ – ☐ = ☐

56 – 33   I will subtract ☐ from both sides of the problem.

56 – 33 = ☐ – ☐ = ☐

67 – 24   I will subtract ☐ from both sides of the problem.

67 – 24 = ☐ – ☐ = ☐

89 – 71   I will subtract ☐ from both sides of the problem.

89 – 71 = ☐ – ☐ = ☐

94 – 52   I will subtract ☐ from both sides of the problem.

94 – 52 = ☐ – ☐ = ☐

Two-Digit Regrouping

Use regrouping to solve these problems. The first one is done for you.

	Tens	Ones
	3 ~~4~~	~~6~~ 16
–	2	7
=	1	9

I can't take 7 from 6, so I borrow 10 from 40

16 – 7 = 9

The tens column subtraction is now:

30 – 20 = 10   So, 46 – 27 = 19

	Tens	Ones
	5	5
–	2	6
=		

I can't take 6 from 5, so I borrow 10 from ☐

☐ – 6 = ☐

The tens column subtraction is now:

☐ – 20 = ☐   So, 55 – 26 = ☐

	Tens	Ones
	8	3
–	4	5
=		

I can't take 5 from 3, so I borrow 10 from ☐

☐ – 5 = ☐

The tens column subtraction is now:

☐ – 40 = ☐   So, 83 – 45 = ☐

Solve the problems with regrouping. The first one is done for you.

$$\begin{array}{r} {}^5\!\not6\!\not5{}^{15} \\ -\ 37 \\ \hline 28 \end{array}$$

$$\begin{array}{r} 94 \\ -\ 47 \\ \hline \end{array}$$

$$\begin{array}{r} 77 \\ -\ 48 \\ \hline \end{array}$$

$$\begin{array}{r} 42 \\ -\ 15 \\ \hline \end{array}$$

$$\begin{array}{r} 74 \\ -\ 37 \\ \hline \end{array}$$

$$\begin{array}{r} 66 \\ -\ 29 \\ \hline \end{array}$$

Three-Digit Regrouping

Solve the problems to practice three-digit subtraction using regrouping.

```
  2 13 12
  3̶4̶2̶        534        647        777
– 155      – 247      – 429      – 488
─────      ─────      ─────      ─────
  187
```

```
  475        925        463        614
– 387      – 336      – 273      – 325
─────      ─────      ─────      ─────
```

```
  548        724        548        884
– 255      – 456      – 479      – 326
─────      ─────      ─────      ─────
```

```
  273        371
–  77      – 274
─────      ─────
```

```
  956        184
– 766      –  96
─────      ─────
```

Word Problems

Solve the word problems and show your work in the box.

15 children were in the park. Then 8 had to go home. How many were left?

A shop had 16 soccer balls. On Monday, it sold 4. On Tuesday, it sold 6. How many were left?

A school had 60 students. Half of them left on a field trip. How many were in class?

64 children signed up for dance classes. During the year, 19 quit. How many were left at the end of the year?

Max had 46 problems to solve. He solved 21 of them. How many did he still need to solve?

56 children reached level 2 in a game. 27 of them also reached level 3. How many only reached level 2?

Prepare for **Division**

Draw pictures to show how you would share the food equally.

Share 10 strawberries evenly among 2 people. Show how many they get each.

Share 6 cookies evenly among 3 people. Show how many they get each.

Share 12 sandwiches evenly among 3 people. Show how many they get each.

Share 12 carrots evenly among 4 people. Show how many they get each.

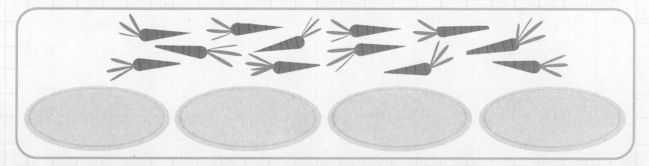

Congruent Shapes

Two shapes of the same size and shape are called congruent shapes. Circle the congruent shapes in each box.

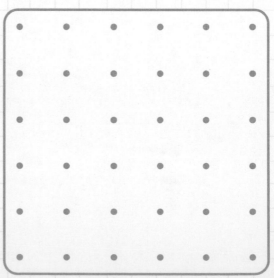

Connect dots in each box to draw a five-sided shape. The two shapes you draw should not be congruent.

Match Shapes

A rectangle has 4 sides. A hexagon has 6 sides.
Shade the rectangles **blue**.
Shade the hexagons **red**.

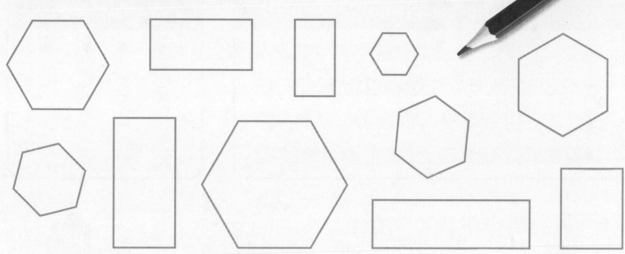

Draw lines to match the text with the shapes.

I have **4** vertices (corners) and
4 straight sides of the same length.

I have **3** straight sides and **3** vertices.
I am symmetrical.

I have **4** vertices and **4** straight sides
that are not all the same length.

I have **5** straight sides and **5** vertices.
I am symmetrical.

I have **8** vertices and **8** straight sides
of the same length.

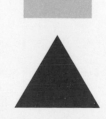

Lines

A horizontal line runs from left to right. A vertical line runs from top to bottom. Trace the lines.

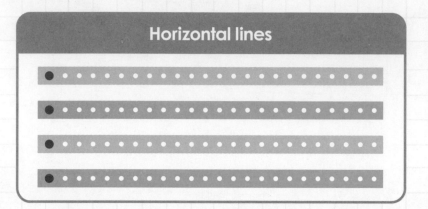

Horizontal lines

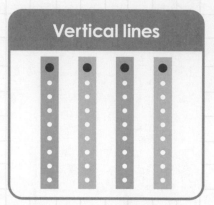

Vertical lines

Decide if each object forms a horizontal (←→) or vertical (↕) line and check the correct box.

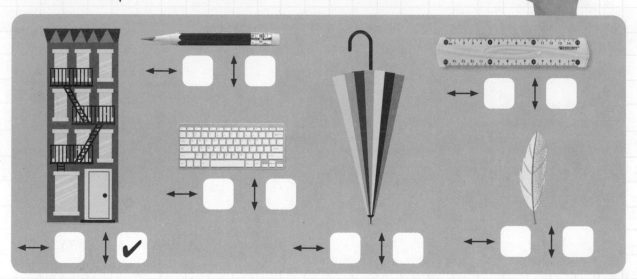

Parallel lines always stay the same distance apart and never meet. Use a ruler to draw a parallel line beside each line.

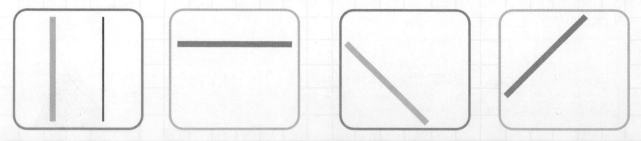

Sort Shapes

Four-sided shapes are called quadrilaterals. Draw lines to sort the quadrilaterals into their types.

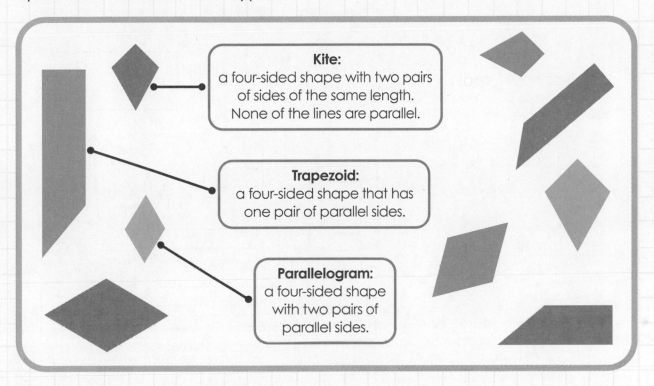

Kite:
a four-sided shape with two pairs of sides of the same length. None of the lines are parallel.

Trapezoid:
a four-sided shape that has one pair of parallel sides.

Parallelogram:
a four-sided shape with two pairs of parallel sides.

Write **T** for true or **F** for false in the box after each sentence.

I have **5** sides. ☐ I have **5** vertices. ☐ I have **3** pairs of equal sides. ☐	**Pentagons**
I have an odd number of sides. ☐ I have **7** vertices. ☐ I have **9** sides. ☐	**Heptagons**
I have **2** vertices. ☐ I have **4** sides. ☐ I am not symmetrical. ☐	**Semicircles**

3D Shapes

Use the key to color the 3D shapes.

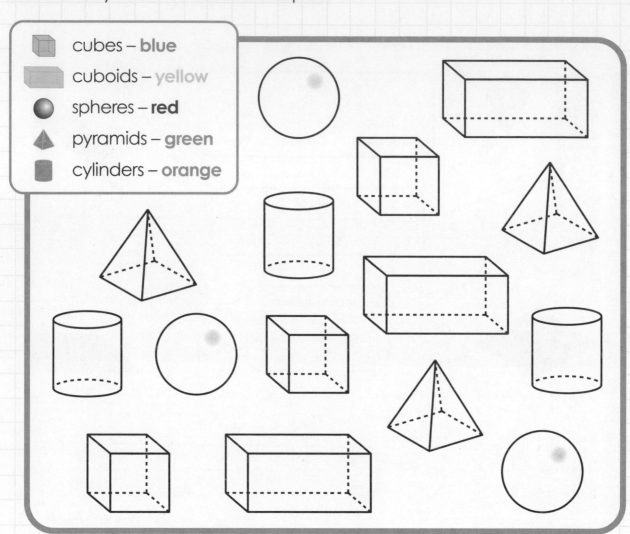

cubes – **blue**

cuboids – yellow

spheres – **red**

pyramids – **green**

cylinders – **orange**

Count the faces on the shapes and write the number.

A cube has **6** faces and **12** edges.

A cuboid has ☐ faces and ☐ edges.

A cylinder has ☐ faces and ☐ edges.

A pyramid has ☐ faces and ☐ edges.

A sphere has ☐ face and ☐ edges.

3D Shapes

Draw lines to match the words, 3D shapes, and objects.

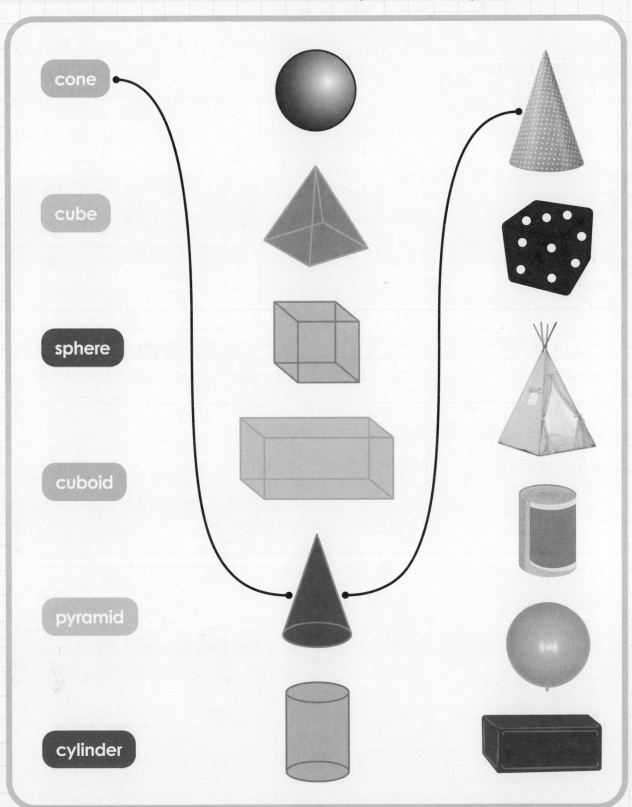

cone

cube

sphere

cuboid

pyramid

cylinder

Graphs

Line graphs show how things change over time. The horizontal line (the x-axis) shows the time. The vertical line (the y-axis) shows the measurement that changes. Use the line graph to answer the questions below.

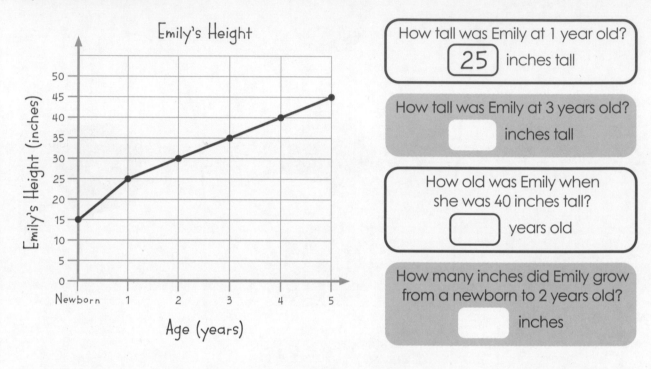

How tall was Emily at 1 year old?
[25] inches tall

How tall was Emily at 3 years old?
[ ] inches tall

How old was Emily when she was 40 inches tall?
[ ] years old

How many inches did Emily grow from a newborn to 2 years old?
[ ] inches

Use the line graph to answer the questions below.

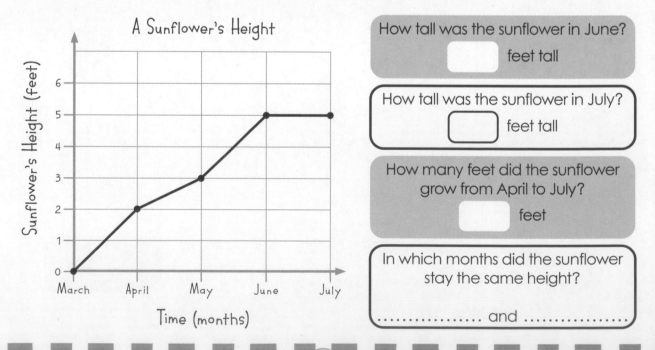

How tall was the sunflower in June?
[ ] feet tall

How tall was the sunflower in July?
[ ] feet tall

How many feet did the sunflower grow from April to July?
[ ] feet

In which months did the sunflower stay the same height?
.... and ....

Graphs

The bar graph shows how many fruits are for sale at the market.
Use the graph to answer the questions.

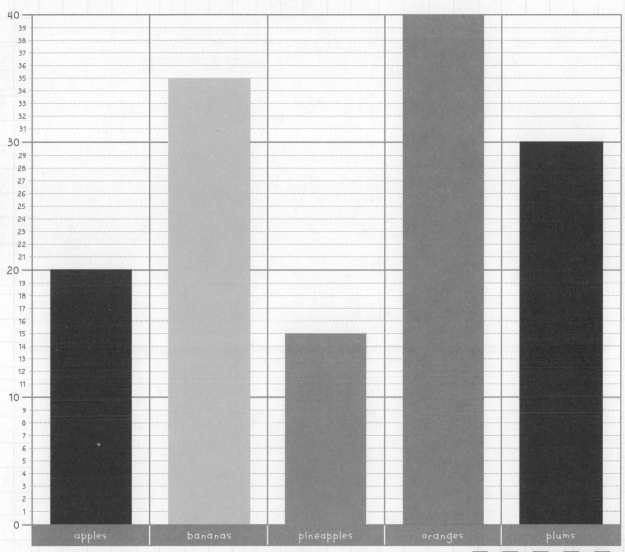

How many types of fruit were for sale? ☐

How many pineapples were for sale? ☐

How many more plums than apples were there? ☐

How many oranges and bananas were for sale in total? ☐

Which fruit did the market have the most of? ....

Which fruit did the market have the fewest of? ....

Fractions

When we split shapes into equal parts, each part is called a fraction. Draw a line to split each shape into two equal halves. Then color one half ($\frac{1}{2}$) of each shape.

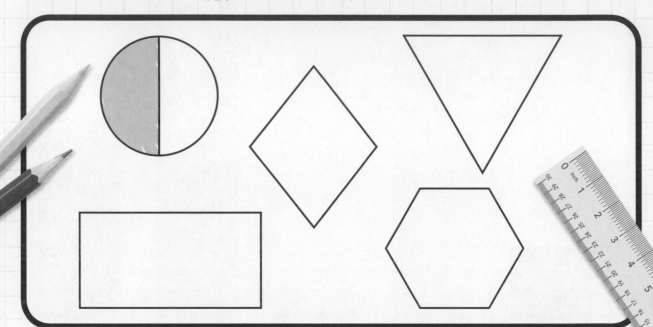

Draw lines to split each shape into three thirds. Then color one third ($\frac{1}{3}$) of each shape.

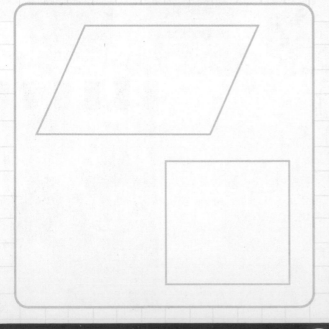

Draw lines to split each shape into four quarters. Then color one quarter ($\frac{1}{4}$) of each shape.

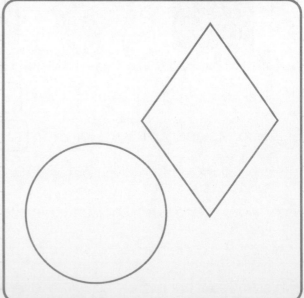

Fractions

The bottom number in a fraction tells you how many parts you need to make a whole. The bottom number of $\frac{1}{3}$ is 3. This means you need 3 thirds to make a whole. Write the answers.

You need ☐ halves ($\frac{1}{2}$s) to make a whole.

You need ☐ thirds ($\frac{1}{3}$s) to make a whole.

You need ☐ quarters ($\frac{1}{4}$s) to make a whole.

Shade $\frac{1}{3}$ **blue**. Shade $\frac{2}{3}$ **red**.

Shade $\frac{3}{3}$ **green**.

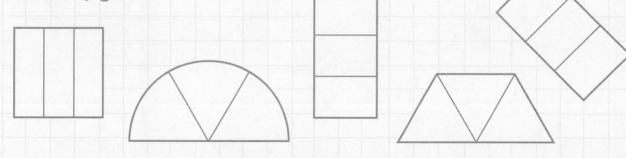

Count how many parts are shaded and complete the fractions.

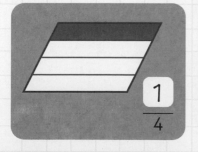
$\frac{1}{4}$

$\frac{\ }{3}$

$\frac{\ }{2}$

$\frac{\ }{4}$

Measure Size

Check the boxes to answer the questions.

Which is taller?

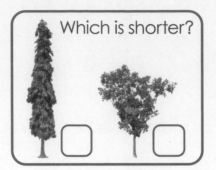
Which is shorter?

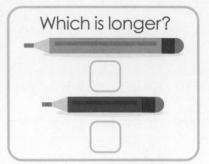
Which is longer?

Which is wider?

Which is smaller?

Which is bigger?

Use a ruler to measure the candies.

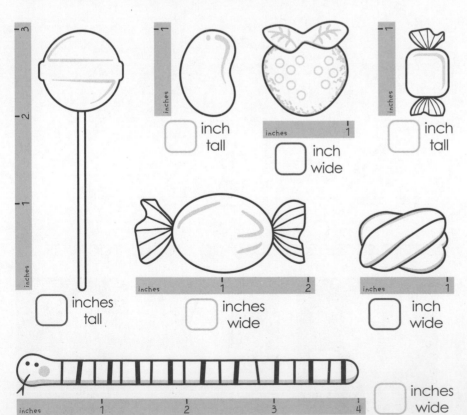

inch tall

inch wide

inch tall

inches tall

inches wide

inch wide

inches wide

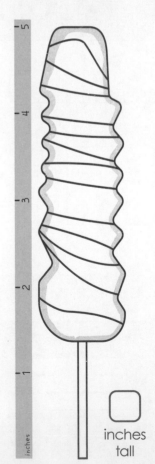

inches tall

Measure Length

We can measure things using objects. Count the objects and write the lengths.

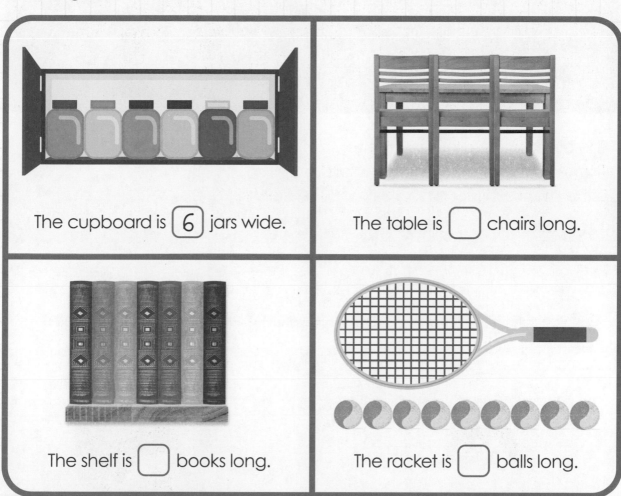

The cupboard is 6 jars wide.

The table is ⬜ chairs long.

The shelf is ⬜ books long.

The racket is ⬜ balls long.

The lizard is 10 inches long. Then it grows 2 more inches. How long is it now?

⬜ **inches**

A sandwich is 8 inches long. If someone eats 4 inches of it, how many inches will be left?

⬜ **inches**

Height

Use the clues to solve the problems. Circle the correct answers.

Carl is the same height as Sophia.
Sophia is shorter than Tom.
Is Tom taller or shorter than Carl?

taller   **shorter**

The elephant is taller than the lion.
The monkey is shorter than the lion.
Is the monkey taller or shorter than the elephant?

taller   **shorter**

We often measure people in feet (ft). 1 foot is 12 inches (in).
Use the height charts to measure each child or animal's height
in feet.

[ ] ft   [ ] ft   [ ] ft   [ ] ft   [ ] ft   [ ] ft

Volume

Circle the item in each pair that contains more than the other.

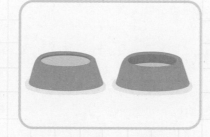

Color in the measuring cups to show the liquid.

1 cup	**3 cups**	**2 cups**
orange juice	tomato juice	apple juice

How many cups are in 1 pint? 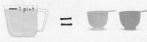 .... cups

How many pints are in 1 quart?   .... pints

How many cups are in 1 quart?  .... cups

Temperature

Which is hotter?

Which is colder?

A thermometer tells us how hot or cold something is. Write the temperatures on the thermometers.

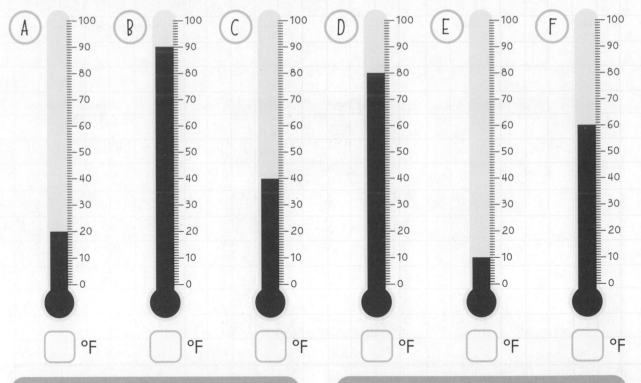

A [ ] °F B [ ] °F C [ ] °F D [ ] °F E [ ] °F F [ ] °F

Which thermometer shows the coldest temperature? ....

Which thermometer shows the hottest temperature? ....

Weight

Circle the heaviest object in each pair.

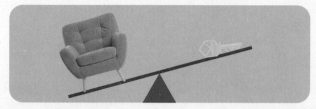

Draw lines to match each object to one of the weight categories.

400 lb

10 lb

99 lb

35 lb

200 lb

Weighs **more than** 100 pounds (lb)

Weighs **less than** 100 pounds (lb)

1 lb

20 lb

250 lb

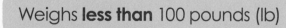

50 lb

140 lb

Clock Work

We use a clock to tell the time. The short hand shows the hour. The long hand shows the minutes. Complete the sentences.

 It is ...**four**... o'clock.

 It is quarter-past ....

 It is half-past ....

 It is quarter to ....

Draw the hands on the clocks.

two o'clock

half-past seven

quarter to ten

The hours from midnight through the morning to midday, or noon, are known as a.m. The hours from midday through the afternoon and evening to midnight are known as p.m. Circle the answers.

2:00 p.m.   2:00 a.m.

7:00 a.m.   10:00 p.m.

11:00 p.m.   9:00 a.m.

Time

On a digital clock, the time is written in numbers. 10:00 means ten o'clock, and 10:30 means half-past ten. What times do these digital clocks show?

..... one .....
..... o'clock .....

....

....

....

....

....

....

....

Write the times on the watches.

one o'clock

half-past five

quarter-past six

quarter to eight

What time do you have breakfast?

What time do you go to school?

What time is noon?

What time do you go to bed?

My Community

A **community** is made up of many different people, such as teachers, friends, and family. Some people, such as firefighters, provide important services.

Finish these sentences about your community.

The people in my family are called ....

....

My teacher is called ....

....

My friends are called ....

....

Draw some of the people in your community.
You could include garbage collectors, postal workers, and other people you know. Write their names underneath.

....

Different Communities

> The people living in the center of busy towns or cities make up **urban** communities.

> People living in spread-out suburbs make up **suburban** communities.

> Those living in the country make up **rural** communities.

Circle the kind of community you live in.

Urban

Suburban

Rural

Circle the community where you are most likely to see each object.

urban   rural
suburban

urban   rural
suburban

urban   rural
suburban

urban   rural
suburban

urban   rural
suburban

urban   rural
suburban

Write down two objects from the pictures above that are in your community.

....

....

Jobs and Activities

Read about the differences between rural, suburban, and urban communities. Underline key words in each paragraph.

Rural Communities

The open land in rural areas is often used for growing crops or raising farm animals. People either live in farmhouses or in small towns with only a few houses and stores.

Urban Communities

There are lots of factories and offices in urban communities, which provide many jobs. People who live here travel using trains, buses, and taxis.

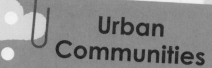

Suburban Communities

Suburban homes often have a small backyard. There are parks and small shopping centers. People who live in the suburbs often travel into cities and towns for work.

Circle the jobs that people do in your community.

firefighter	teacher	factory worker	farmer
office worker	waiter	doctor	garbage collector
builder	fisherman	bus driver	mechanic

Write a sentence about a job you would like to have. Say why you like it.

....

....

Climates

An area's **climate** is its weather pattern over a long time. To learn about a climate, scientists measure things such as temperature, wind, and rain patterns over many years.

Write the name of each climate under its picture.

Polar climates are very cold and dry all year round.

Dry climates are very hot and dry all year round.

Tropical climates are hot and damp all year round.

Mild climates have dry, hot summers and mild, wet winters.

Continental climates have hot summers and cold winters.

....

....

Write two sentences about the climate where you live.

....

....

My Home

People live in different types of homes.
Write the correct label under each image.

> houseboat   apartment   trailer   house

Draw your home.

Write two sentences describing your home.

Different Homes

Around the world, people build houses to suit their climate. Draw a line to match each image to its description.

Southeast Asia has a wet, tropical climate. This house is built on stilts to protect it from flood waters.

Some parts of East Africa have a very hot, wet climate. The roof of this house is made from cool, waterproof cow dung.

Rainwater runs easily from sloped roofs, and bricks keep out cold and heat. This works well for people in mild climates.

Some parts of northern Africa have a very hot, dry climate. This house is built underground to protect people from the heat.

How is your home suited to your climate?

....

....

....

Community Features

People build communities near **natural resources**, such as rivers.
They build **human-made resources**, such as hospitals, in their communities.
We use symbols on maps to help us find these resources.

Draw a line to match the name of each symbol to its picture.

mountains	river	national park	hospital

school	airport	train station	store

Think of a feature of your community, such as a bus station.
Create a symbol for it here.

Map Grids

Use the grid references to find the places. Go along the base to find the letter and go up the side to find the number.

Map Key:

airport   hospital   national park   river   mountains   school

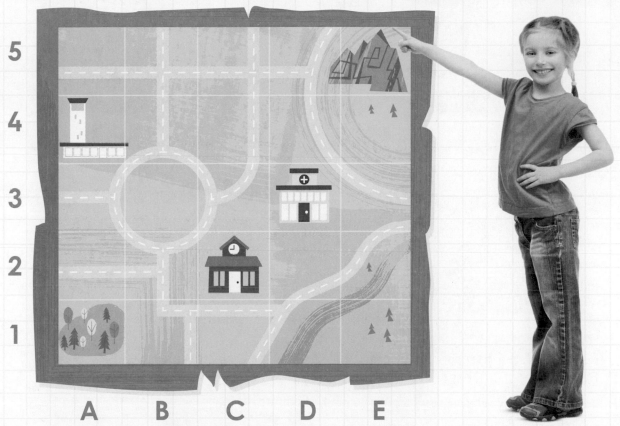

Which building is in D3? ....

Which building is in square C2? ....

Which natural feature is in square A1? ....

Which natural resource is in squares D1 and E2? ....

Which building is in A4? ....

What is a Compass?

A compass helps people figure out which direction they need to travel in. Write the directions on the compass below.

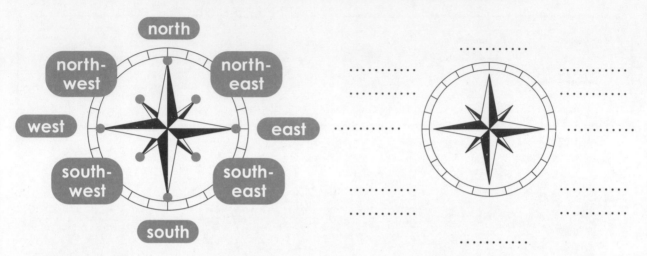

north

north-west

north-east

west

east

south-west

south-east

south

Look at the map, and then fill in the sentences below with north, south, east, or west.

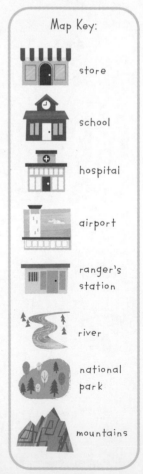

Map Key:

store

school

hospital

airport

ranger's station

river

national park

mountains

The store is .... of the school.

The hospital is .... of the airport.

The ranger's station is .... of the national park.

The river is .... of the mountains.

Follow **Directions**

Use the map to answer the questions below.

Which building is three squares east of the park?

....

Which building is two squares north of the library?

....

Which building is one square south of the post office?

....

Which building is three squares west of the hospital?

....

Which building is two squares north and two squares east of the park?

....

Which building is one square north and three squares west of the store?

....

SOCIAL STUDIES

The Continents

A **continent** is a large area of land. There are seven continents. Most of the continents are divided up into countries.

Shade Europe in **purple**.

Shade Africa in green.

Shade Asia in yellow.

Shade Antarctica in **blue**.

Shade Australia in orange.

Shade North America in **pink**.

Shade South America in **red**.

Which continent do you live in?

....

....

The Ocean

Earth has four ocean basins: **Pacific Ocean**, **Indian Ocean**, **Atlantic Ocean**, and **Arctic Ocean**. They all link up to form one global ocean.

Find each ocean on the map, and then finish the sentence below.

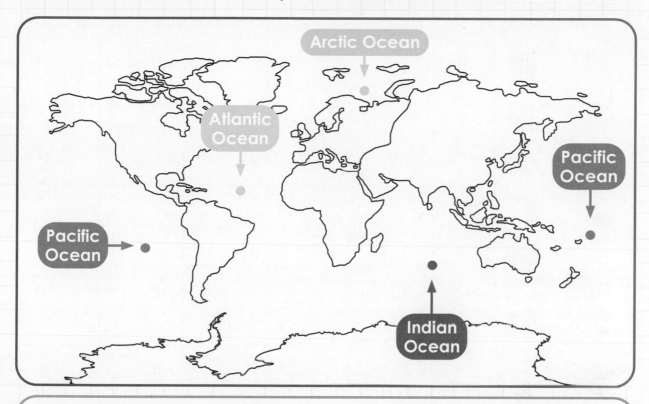

The ocean nearest my home is the .... Ocean.

Unscramble the letters to make an ocean word. Then find the words in the word search.

PFCAICI ....

NDINAI ....

LNATICAT ....

CRITAC ....

C	R	E	P	A	C	I	F	I	C
A	R	E	O	C	F	U	G	T	I
D	T	H	I	L	I	T	I	I	C
E	I	L	I	A	U	K	V	N	A
A	C	B	A	G	R	U	C	D	I
J	I	P	D	N	U	Z	A	I	P
A	G	W	R	A	T	R	J	A	I
G	U	V	Y	X	P	I	M	N	K
A	R	C	T	I	C	P	C	O	J
U	C	A	R	T	E	A	C	U	T

Population

The **population** is the number of people or animals in an area. Scientists count populations to see if they are growing, getting smaller, or staying the same.

On the chart, color one square for each animal.

5					
4					
3					
2					
1					

leopard   snake   toucan   frog   orangutan

Answer the questions below.

Which type of animal has the largest population?

....

Which type of animal has the smallest population?

....

Which two populations are the same size?

....

212

The Environment

Our actions affect the environment in positive and negative ways. Read about these two negative actions and answer the questions.

Cutting down many trees is called **deforestation**. Many animals die from deforestation because their home, or habitat, is destroyed.

When we throw away plastic items, such as bottles, we create **plastic pollution**. If it isn't recycled, it ends up in landfill or in the oceans. Animals can swallow the plastic or become trapped in it.

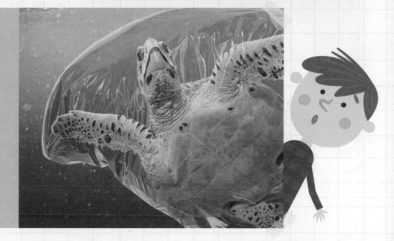

Why is deforestation harmful to the environment?

....

....

Why is plastic pollution harmful to the environment?

....

....

Write about positive ways you can prevent deforestation and plastic pollution.

....

....

....

....

My Timeline

People change over time. We can show these changes on a timeline. Write your own timeline below. Choose from the events in the box or others that have happened to you.

When you started school.

When a brother or sister was born.

When you moved to a new house.

When you met your best friend.

When you went on vacation.

Top Tip:
Write the date and year when events happened.

I was born!

What is a Biography?

A **biography** is a text written about someone else's life. It tells you about events that have happened in their life.

Read the biography below and answer the questions.

Malala Yousafzai

Malala Yousafzai was born on July 12, 1997. In 2008, Taliban rulers in Pakistan said that girls could not go to school anymore. Malala started writing a blog about girls' rights to go to school. In 2012, Malala was shot by a Taliban gunman, but she survived. Malala and her family moved to the United Kingdom, and she created a charity to help all girls have the opportunity for education. She received a Nobel Peace Prize in 2014.

In what year was Malala born?

....

In 2008, what did the Taliban rulers say?

....

What type of charity did Malala set up?

....

What prize did Malala receive in 2014?

....

Inside the Earth

Read the facts below, and use them to help you label this cross section of Earth. Then color it in.

> The thinnest layer is the **crust**, which covers the Earth's surface.

> The **mantle** is in the middle, between the core and the crust.

> The **core** is a large metal ball at Earth's center.

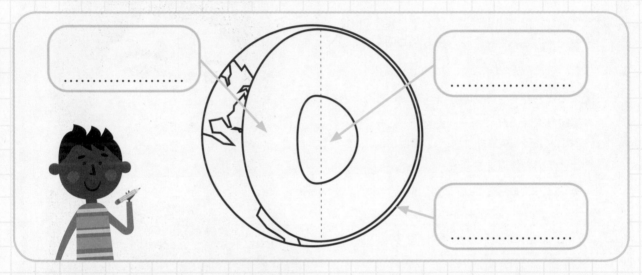

We live on continents (large blocks of land) that float on top of the mantle. Look at the diagram, and color the mantle orange, the soil brown, the continental crust green, and the ocean blue.

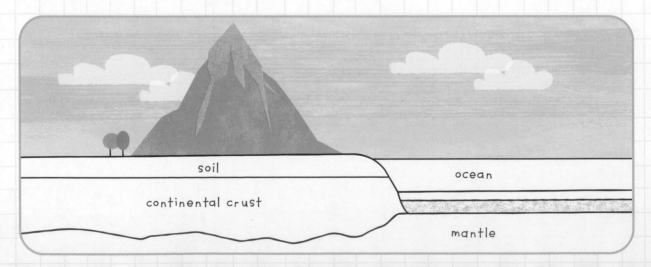

Types of Rock

There are three main types of rock: **sedimentary**, **metamorphic**, and **igneous**.

Read about each type of rock, and answer the questions below.

Sedimentary

Sedimentary rocks are made of sand, shells, pebbles, and other materials cemented together in layers. Sometimes we see fossils in these rocks.

Metamorphic

Metamorphic rocks form under great heat and pressure inside the Earth. They have smooth layers and can contain crystals.

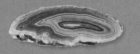

Igneous

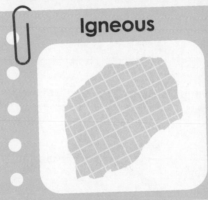

Igneous rocks form when volcanic lava cools. They can be smooth and shiny, or bubbly and filled with holes.

In which type of rock might you find a fossil? ....

Which type of rock would you find near a volcano? ....

In which type of rock might you find crystals? ....

Which type of rock is sometimes filled with tiny bubbles? ....

In which rock would you find smooth layers? ....

Water Cycle

The **water cycle** shows the movement of Earth's water. It explains how we get **clouds**, **rain**, and **rivers**.

Read the meanings of the terms below, and then write them in the correct places on the diagram.

Precipitation: when water falls to Earth as rain or snow.

Collection: when water collects in a river, lake, or ocean.

Evaporation: when water turns into an invisible vapor, or gas, and rises into the sky.

Condensation: when water vapor cools into tiny water droplets. These droplets form clouds.

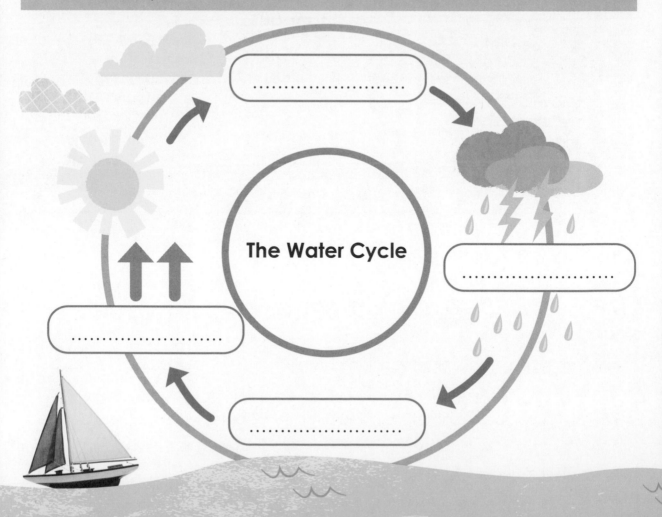

The Water Cycle

Clouds

There are three main types of cloud: cirrus, cumulus, and stratus. Draw a line to match each description to the correct picture.

cumulus

Fluffy, mostly white, look like cotton candy, found low in the sky.

cirrus

Thin, feathery clouds, found very high in the sky.

stratus

Wispy, mostly gray clouds hanging low in the sky.

Look at the sky above you, today. Draw any clouds you see in the box below.

Liquid, Solid, or Gas?

Water has three different states: liquid, solid, and gas.

Read the definitions of these states, and then write some examples.

Type	Definition	Example
liquid	Liquid water is wet and can be poured.	a river
solid	Solid water is ice.	
gas	Water in gas form is invisible. It is called water vapor.	

Fill in the missing labels on the diagram below to show how water changes between the different states of matter.

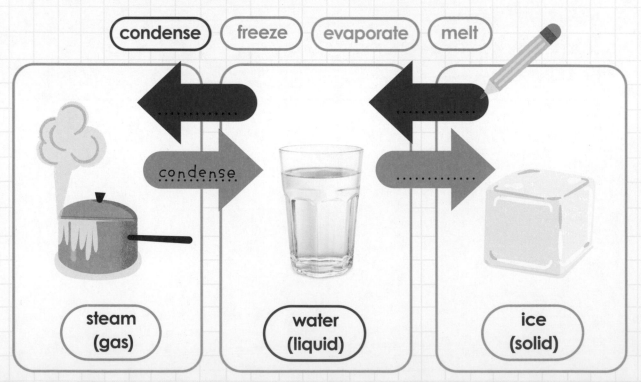

condense   freeze   evaporate   melt

condense

steam
(gas)

water
(liquid)

ice
(solid)

Plants

Label the different parts of the plant. Then draw lines to link the labels with their functions.

(fruit) (leaves) (roots) (stem) (**flower**)

Produces seeds and has bright petals to attract insects.

Uses light to make food.

Holds up the plant and transports food and water.

Takes in water and minerals from the soil.

Contains seeds and is eaten by animals and people.

Life Cycles

Label each stage of the butterfly life cycle, and then fill in the blanks in the text below.

(caterpillar) (chrysalis) (egg) (butterfly)

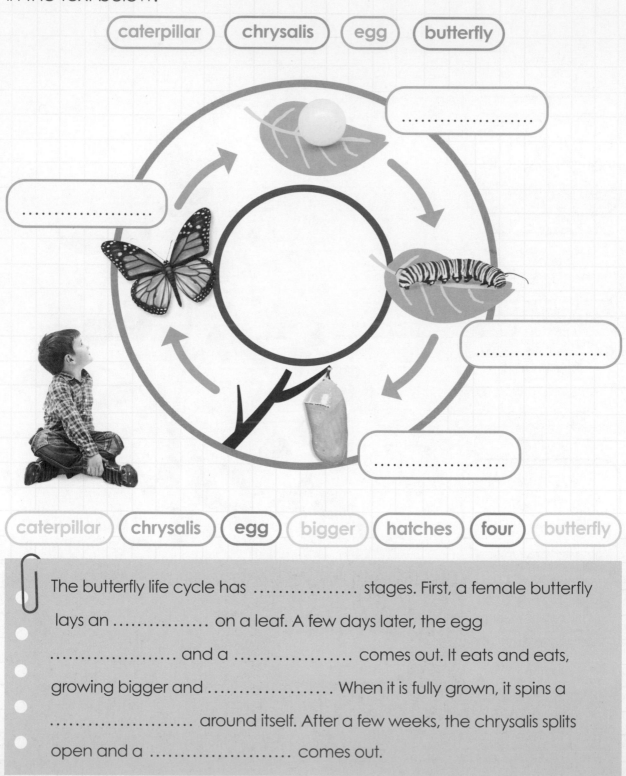

(caterpillar) (chrysalis) (egg) (bigger) (hatches) (four) (butterfly)

The butterfly life cycle has .... stages. First, a female butterfly lays an .... on a leaf. A few days later, the egg .... and a .... comes out. It eats and eats, growing bigger and .... When it is fully grown, it spins a .... around itself. After a few weeks, the chrysalis splits open and a .... comes out.

Creepy Crawlies

Honeybees are important insects. They help plants produce fruit. Label the parts of this honeybee.

(abdomen) (antennae) (leg) (wings) (head) (thorax)

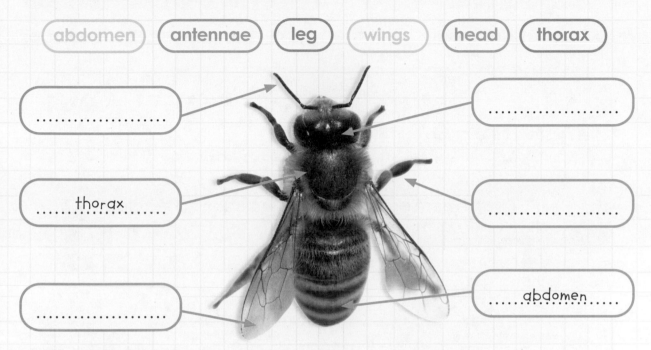

....

.... thorax ....

.... abdomen ....

....

....

Unscramble these names to reveal some other helpful creepy crawlies.

gubdyla	....	This spotted insect eats up lots of plant pests, such as aphids.
pswa	....	This striped, buzzing insect enjoys eating pests that feed on vegetables.
nogdralyf	....	This colorful flying insect feasts on plant pests.
owmr	....	This long, wiggly creature helps to break down leaves and grass into soil.

Grouping Animals

Scientists divide animals with backbones into five groups: **mammals**, **birds**, **fish**, **reptiles**, and **amphibians**.

Read about the groups, and then sticker the correct group name.

_____ have hair or fur, give birth to live young, and feed their babies milk.

_____ hatch from eggs. They have a beak and feathers. Most of them can fly.

_____ usually hatch from eggs. Most live on land and have scaly skin.

_____ usually hatch from eggs and live part of their lives in water and part on land. They have slimy skin.

_____ usually hatch from eggs. They live in water, breathe through gills, and have scales.

Where Do I Belong?

Write which group each animal belongs to and two reasons why.

tiger	alligator	bear
A tiger is a	An alligator is a	A bear is a ....
I know this because	I know this because	I know this because ....

shark	eagle	frog
A shark is a	An eagle is a	A frog is an ....
I know this because	I know this because	I know this because ....

The Human Life Cycle

Number the pictures 1 to 6 to put them in the correct order.
Write some words to describe the people at each stage.

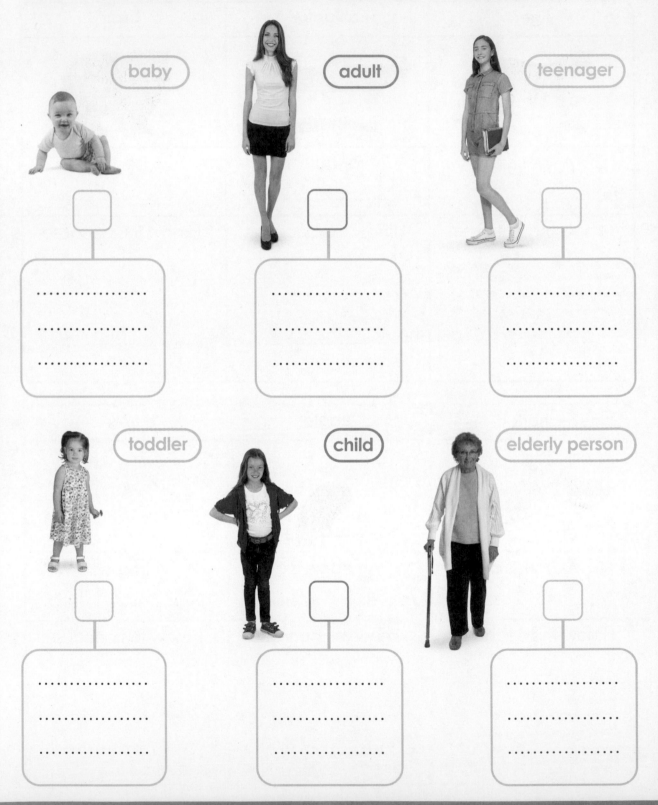

baby

adult

teenager

toddler

child

elderly person

The Human Body

Draw arrows from the organs to where they are found in the body.

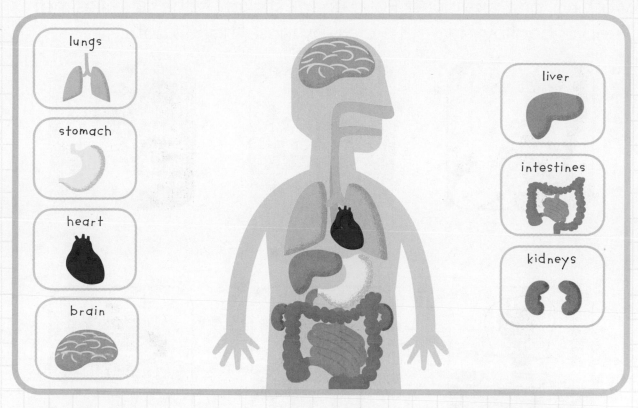

Follow the lines to match the organ to its function. Then fill in the correct word.

stomach

kidneys

liver

brain

lungs

heart

intestines

The .... clean the blood and make urine.

The .... breaks up the food we eat into tiny pieces.

We use our .... to breathe.

The .... helps break food into even smaller pieces.

The .... is used for thinking and memory.

The .... take the nutrients from food into our body.

The .... pumps blood around the body.

Staying Healthy

We keep our bodies working well by eating healthy foods, washing, and exercising. Put a check sticker by the activities that keep us healthy, and put a cross by those that do not.

Fruits and vegetables are healthy foods. Fried foods and foods with lots of sugar are not so healthy. Circle the foods that help keep us healthy.

Simple Machines

We use simple machines to make jobs easier. Draw lines to match the simple machines with their meanings.

wedge

A slanting flat surface.

screw

One or more wheels with a rod through the center.

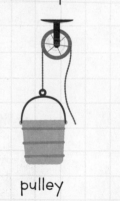

inclined plane

An object with a thick end and a pointed end.

A ramp that winds around a cylinder.

pulley

lever

A straight bar that pivots about a single point.

wheel and axle

A rope or chain that rolls around a wheel.

Friction

Friction is a **force** between two surfaces that are touching.
The more **friction** there is, the slower an object moves.
The more **friction** there is, the less slippery a surface is.

Circle the picture in each pair where there is more friction.

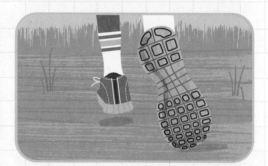

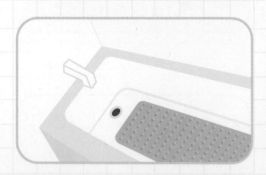 

Magnets

A **magnet** is a piece of **metal** that can pull other metal objects toward itself. The force of magnets, called **magnetism**, is a **natural force**.

Write the correct words in the sentences.

(**poles**)　(push)　(**repel**)　(north)　(**pull**)　(south)

The ends of magnets are called .... One end is the

.... pole and the other is the .... pole.

When we put opposite poles near each other, they .... toward each other. We say the poles attract.

When we put the same poles near each other, they .... away from each other. We say the poles ....

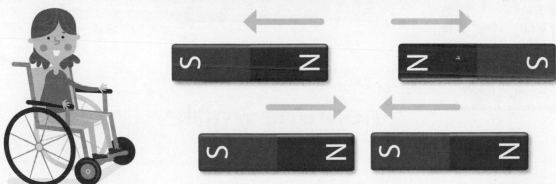

Circle the objects the magnet will attract.

Energy Sources

Renewable energy, such as wind power, cannot be used up because it comes from natural sources. Nonrenewable energy, such as coal and oil, comes from fossil fuels and will one day run out.

Draw lines from the objects to the type of energy they use.

renewable

nonrenewable

Using Energy

Write the energy source for each group. Choose from the words below.

(**batteries**) (electric cables) (**fuel**) (human)

....	scissors	bicycle	roller skates
....	car	plane	tractor
....	television	light bulb	toaster
....	remote control	flashlight	toy robot

Look around your home. List the items you can see under the correct energy source.

(**batteries**) (electric cables) (**fuel**) (human)

....	....	....	....
....	....	....	....
....	....	....	....
....	....	....	....

Answers

Handwriting

p4 again, ahead, alphabet, America, astronaut, away

p5 baboon, baby, blubber, blueberry, Brazil, bubble

p6 cactus, catch, China, circus, click, cocoon

p7 dance, December, did, disk, dodge, drive

p9 gaming, garage, garbage, goggles, Greenland

p10 Hawaii, high, hippo, horse, hour, hundred

p12 Kansas, kind, kitchen, knee, knight, know

p13 level, likely, lizard, London, long, loyal

p14 mammal, mermaid, mime, mix, Monday, mouth

p15 never, next, ninja, noise, none, November

p16 October, odd, oil, okay, order, our

p18 race, rain, referee, relax, ruler, Russia

p19 scissors, season, shoes, star, stink, Sunday

p20 taste, tent, that, thirsty, tight, Tuesday

p21 ukulele, under, uniform, use, usual, Utah

p22 van, video, Viking, violin, vote, vulture

p24 year, yellow, Yemen, yes, yesterday, yo-yo

p25 Zanzibar, zap, zebra, zither, zone, zoo

Reading

p26 Max's Wilderness Adventure, Tales of Brave Princesses, Learn the Rules of Football, Rescue at Red Ridge

p27 The main idea of the whole text is that coral reefs are full of colorful fish. The main idea of the second paragraph is that coral reefs are made from the shells of coral polyps. The main idea of the third paragraph is that smaller fish provide food for larger fish in a food chain.

p28 The main idea of the text is that life was very different for children in Ancient Egypt than it is for modern children.

p29 1 a type of flower, 2 quiet and private, 3 fussy, 4 a machine for lifting heavy objects, 5 bounced off, 6 started to grow

p30 Fiction titles: Robbie Rabbit Starts School, Milly the Magical Fairy, Superheroes to the Rescue

p31 1 Mice are much smaller than lions. 2 To repay him for letting her go. 3 A kind deed is never wasted. No one is too small to help others.

p32 1 Why people light red lanterns and fireworks at New Year. 2 Because most people couldn't write. 3 To keep alive an old story.

p33 1 Frida Kahlo was lucky to survive polio and a traffic accident. 3 Subtracting the year she was born from the year she died tells us that she lived about 47 years.

p36 1 The writer wants the family next door to move away and a quieter family to move in. 4 Answers may vary. This might have been written by someone who does not have a family or dog and who likes quiet.

p37 1 This story is based on *The Three Little Pigs*. 2 pigs, wolf 3 Both stories involve three

characters building homes, some of which are destroyed. 4 Taking the time to do things well will pay off in the end.

p38 1 The elephant is tangled up in a telephone cord. 2 elephant/telephant; elephone/ telephone; quite/right; trunk/telephunk; free/telephee; song/telephong 3 telephone/elephant; elephant/telephone; telephone/trunk

p39 1 The child doesn't like having to go to bed when it is still light outside. 2 night/light; way/ day; see/tree; feet/street; you/blue; play/day 3 The poet might have repeated these words to show how strongly he felt. 4 The words "candle light" tell us this poem was written long ago.

p40 1 clay 3 soda, coloring, soap

p42 The problem was that people's shoes were going missing. The thief was a fox. The thief stole shoes. The story took place in suburban Berlin. The man followed the fox to its den. The shoes went missing overnight. No one knows why the fox took the shoes. It may have been the smell.

p43 Answers may vary. Anna saw the sparkling blue ocean. She heard the roaring waves. She felt the coldness of the water. She tasted the salt in the sea. She smelled a barbecue.

p44

	Simile	Metaphor
She runs like a racehorse.	✓	
You are a star!		✓
Their room is a pigsty.		✓
Mia was as quiet as a mouse.	✓	
His brain is a super computer.		✓
She has the heart of a lion.		✓
He growled like a bear.	✓	
The storm struck like a wild beast.	✓	
Her hair is a river of gold.		✓
My bag is as light as a feather.	✓	
My teacher is as busy as a bee.	✓	
His stomach is a bottomless pit.		✓

p45 1 That she was asleep. 2 cold 3 gym 4 He didn't like it. 5 Lizzy had burned her hand. 6 He is on a bike.

Writing

p46 1 short, 2 George is the main character. He is in a sinking boat. 3 If George will be rescued and how.

p47 1 B, 2 A

p48 1 but, 2 so, 3 unless, 4 because, 5 so that, 6 also, 7 Then, 8 either … or

p54 1 They are both about ants. 2 The first text provides information about ants and the second tells readers how to get rid of them. 3 A scientific book or website. 4 A magazine article or website about caring for your home.

Word Study

p66 Activity 1: win/ter 2, um/brel/la 3, cat/er/pil/lar 4, cray/on 2, al/pha/bet 3 Activity 2: 1 syllable: play, kite, 2 syllables: monkey, cupcake, picture, rainbow, robot, 3 syllables: flamingo, family

p67 Activity 1: sk**u**nk, sh**e**d, f**i**sh, dr**o**p Activity 2: **t**ent, **f**rog, **n**est, **d**rum, **p**arro**t**, **b**anana, **a**corn, **p**enguin

p68 Red words: unable, unlock, unafraid, unfriendly, unties, untidy Green words: reread, removes, remember, recycle

p69 replay, unusual, underwater, impossible, invisible, retry, disappear, rewind, nonsense, understand

p70 Activity 1: truthful, fearless, slowest, taller

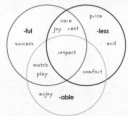

p71 Activity 1: highest, tallest, smallest, powerful, friendship, sickness, playful, colorful Activity 2: power**ful**, friend**ship**, small**est** play**ful**, dark**ness** colorful

p72 Activity 1: overcook/cook; making/make; reread/read; disconnect/connect; undo/ do; watchful/watch; misunderstand/ understand; deserving/deserve Activity 2: stop, cry, like

p73 lipstick, cupcake, grasshopper, rainbow, bedroom, dragonfly, armchair, lighthouse, sunflower

```
g b e d r o o m o n e d
r o n s u n f l o w e r
a e c a b v o i s l n a
s u a b e t c p q i w g
s s o a b s m s u g n o
h s g p u c t a h a n
o r m c h a i r t i f
p w e x f a h c a h n l
p e r d g h k k i o b y
e i a g o n f e b u o e
r s n o w m a n n s w l
o p d r o o f u w e y u
```

p74 Activity 1: Answers may vary: tiny, start, see, honest, speedy, scared, chuckle Activity 2: 1 sleepy, 2 huge, 3 adored, 4 shouted, 5 noisy

p75 Activity 1: sad, joyful; slow, quick; quiet, noisy; awake, sleeping; dull, fun Activity 2: sit, stand A; cold, chilly S; tiny, small S; throw, catch A; calm, relax S; high, low A; big, large S; happy, sad A; listen, hear S

p76 the grass, the sun, roses, a mouse, a fish, a lion

p77

She is as strong as an ox.	simile
My watch is as light as a feather.	simile
She has a heart of gold.	metaphor
The chocolate tastes like velvet.	simile
The sisters are two peas in a pod.	metaphor
You are a wise owl.	metaphor
He laughs like a hyena.	simile
They ran like the wind.	simile
The bunny is as white as snow.	simile
The clouds are fluffy marshmallows.	metaphor

p78 Activity 1: weight/wait, eye/I, nose/knows, bear/bare, two/too, for/four, tail/tale, see/sea Activity 2: sale, bee, won, pair, flour

p79 Activity 1: to move in the sky, something that you watch as it happens, a looped ribbon

Activity 2: Answers may vary: to look at something/a timepiece worn on the wrist; the opposite of left/to be correct; to phone someone/jewelry worn on a finger; a night-flying mammal/a special stick for hitting a ball

p80 Activity 1: loud lion; happy hippo; red rocket; playful puppy; delicious dessert; dazzling diamond; sweet smile; kind, kitten
Activity 2: tiny turtle; careful cat crept; pink pig, muddy mess; Flo's favorite, strawberry sundae; Max made, tasty tomato

p81 Activity 1: surprised, angry, happy, proud, confused, worried, sad

p83 Dinosaurs roamed the Earth more than 66 million years ago. Some were herbivores and others were carnivores. Today, scientists study fossils to find out more about how dinosaurs lived.

Grammar and Punctuation

p84 Activity 1: **2** Tim and Tom, **3** my class, **4** That oak tree, **5** our teacher, **6** Their family
Activity 2: **2** Tom, **3** My parents, **4** This building, **5** I, **6** T. rex

p85 Activity 1: **2** babies, **3** stories, **4** families, **5** flies, **6** cities
Activity 2: **2** dresses, **3** dishes, **4** lunches, **5** bosses, **6** boxes
Activity 3: **2** shelves, **3** wives, **4** loaves, **5** lives, **6** halves

p86 one tooth/two teeth; one child/two children; one person; two people; one deer/two deer; one goose/two geese; one man/two men; one sheep/two sheep; one woman/two women; one foot/two feet; one fish/two fish; one fungus/two fungi

p87 **2** Emily, **3** Texas, **4** Friday, **5** New Year, **6** July

p88 Activity 1: laughed, liked, looked, landed, closed, baked, painted
Activity 2: **2** My mom **arrived** to pick us up.
3 Riley **kicked** the ball into the goal.
4 I **asked** my dad to help me build a treehouse.
5 We **looked** everywhere for Jo's lost glasses.
6 He **crossed** the road to get to the park.

p89 **2** will catch, **3** will go, **4** will start, **5** will laugh, **6** will ride

p90 Activity 1:

Past Tense	Present Tense	Future Tense
asked	ask	will ask
called	**call**	will call
loved	love	will love
talked	**talk**	**will talk**
moved	move	**will move**

Activity 2: **1** past, future; **2** past, future, present; **3** future, present, past; **4** past, future, present

p91 Activity 1: **2** fried, **3** spied, **4** copied, **5** tried, **6** replied
Activity 2: **2** drew, **3** went, **4** found, **5** wrote, **6** slept, **7** won, **8** made, **9** ran, **10** did

p92 **2** A brave superhero rescued the tiny baby.
3 The clumsy man dropped the glass vase.
4 I put two cheese sandwiches in my lunch box. **5** The noisy audience couldn't hear the singer's quiet voice. **6** The crowded hall was full of excited children.

p93 Activity 1: **2** loudly, **3** carefully, **4** bravely, **5** quickly, **6** peacefully
Activity 2: here, where; gently how;

yesterday, when; outside, where; soon, when; quietly, how; today, when; everywhere, where; later, when

p94 **2** Olivia did her homework straight away. Then she watched TV. **3** I like carrots and peas, but I don't like cauliflower. **4** Madison worked hard, so her mom gave her a reward. **5** Noah was happy because his friends were coming to visit. **6** We went swimming and we rode our bikes. **7** First, I fed the dog. Then I took him for a walk.
8 She wore a coat because it was cold.

p95 Activity 1: Blue words: **2** Mike, **3** You, **4** We, **5** The wild beast, **6** she
Green words: **2** himself, **3** yourselves, **4** ourselves, **5** itself, **6** herself
Activity 2: **1** itself, **2** themselves, **3** ourselves, **4** herself, **5** myself, **6** himself

p96 Activity 1: **2** You will find his faithful dog by his chair. **3** We crept past the sleeping baby on tiptoes. **4** My mom goes for a run every morning.
Activity 2: **2** At daybreak, we started hiking. **3** In the forest, we saw some deer. **4** When riding your bike, always wear a helmet.

p97 **2** The teacher shut the door. **3** Emily read the book. **4** Many people saw our play. **5** Harry baked the cake. **6** A green alien flew the UFO. **7** The cat watched the mouse. **8** Joe threw the ball into the hoop.

p98 **2** Are you able to help me? Help me! I would like you to help me. **3** What a mess! This room is very messy. Why is this room such a mess? **4** I think a bug has bitten me. Has a bug bitten me? Ouch! **5** How exciting! I feel excited about it. Are you excited, too? **6** Are you free to come over here? I would like it if you came over here. Come here!

p99 Activity 1: you're: you are; I'm: I am; they'll: they will, can't: can not; we've: we have
Activity 2: are not: aren't, I will: I'll, we are: we're, it is: it's, I have: I've

p100 Activity 1: the woman's house, the boy's nose, Sophie's ideas, the bag's handles, Harry's cake
Activity 2: **2** The book's cover is ripped. The books are over there. **3** The singers are ready for the show. The singer's voice is very loud. **4** The dinosaur's baby hatched from an egg. The dinosaurs lived long ago.

p101 Activity 1: the carrots' tops, the horses' tails, the trucks' horns, the monsters' fur, the writers' stories, the boys' wishes, the crabs' claws, the babies' rattles, the bosses' office
Activity 2: the women's team, the children's bikes; the mice's cheese, the teeth's cavities, the people's homes, the fungi's colors, the cacti's spines, the geese's eggs, the sheep's wool

Spelling

p102 Activity 2: house, door, windows, yard, street, town/city

p103 Activity 1: after, cold, right, last, close

p104 Activity 2: The rabbit squeezed <u>under</u> the fence to get <u>inside</u> the garden.
The spider crawled <u>behind</u> the curtain.
The dolls are kept <u>above</u> the books.
"Let's go <u>inside</u>," said Fran. "It's too hot <u>outside</u>."
Our car is parked <u>between</u> the red and the blue car.

p108 climb, write, **g**nat, **k**nee, com**b**, **k**nife, **g**naw, crum**b**

p109
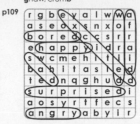

p111 Activity 1: Mon**day**, Tues**day**, Wednes**day**, Thurs**day**, Fri**day**, Satur**day**, Sun**day**
Activity 2: Monday, Thursday, Friday, Sunday

p112 Activity 2: season, summer, year, winter, spring, fall

p113
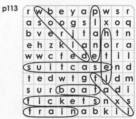

p114 Activity 2: rainy, sunny, snowy, windy, cloudy

p115 Activity 1: sun + flower, paint + brush, ear + ring, rain + bow

p116

p117 Activity 2: station, information, motion, question, invitation, direction

p118 Activity 1: swam, saw, heard, did, slept, made, gave

Counting to 1000

p120

p121 Activity 2: 5 hundreds = 500; 7 hundreds = 700; 1 hundred = 100, 10 hundreds = 1000

p122 Activity 1: 115, 120, 125, 130, 135, 140, 145, 150, 155, 160, 165, 170, 175, 180, 185, 190, 195
Activity 2: 360, 365, 370, 375, 380, 385, 390, 395, 400, 405, 410, 415, 420, 425, 430, 435, 440, 445

p123 Activity 1: 220, 230, 240, 250, 260, 270, 280
Activity 2: 470, 480, 490, 500, 510, 520, 530, 540

p124 Activity 2: 300, 400, 500, 600, 700, 800, 900, 1000

p125 3 tens + 5 ones = 35; 5 tens + 6 ones = 56; 2 tens + 3 ones = 23; 6 tens = 60; 1 ten + 2 ones = 12; 4 tens + 2 ones = 42; 10 tens = 1000

p126 3 hundreds + 2 tens + 5 ones = 325; 2 hundreds + 4 tens + 6 ones = 246; 3 hundreds + 0 tens + 8 ones = 308; 2 hundreds + 5 tens + 0 ones = 250

p127

	hundreds	tens	units
473	4	7	3
826	8	2	6
555	5	5	5
321	3	2	1
835	8	3	5
840	8	4	0
911	9	1	1
703	7	0	3
663	6	6	3
900	9	0	0

p128 734: 4 = ones, 7 = hundreds, 3 = tens
462: 4 = hundreds, 2 = ones, 6 = tens
614: 6 = hundreds, 1 = tens, 4 = ones
570: 0 = ones, 7 = tens, 5 = hundreds
361: 3 = hundreds, 1 = ones, 6 = tens
908: 0 = tens, 9 = hundreds, 8 = ones
800: 8 = hundreds, 0 = tens, 0 = ones

p129

	Place Value	Value
5**2**7	hundreds	500
7**3**4	tens	30
82**4**	ones	4
4**7**5	tens	70
60**3**	ones	3
983	hundreds	900
2**6**0	tens	60
14**2**	ones	2
372	hundreds	300
89**4**	tens	0

p130 Activity 1: 42, 99, 25, 50, 84, 50, 36, 67, 43, 89, 55
Activity 2: 10, 53, 42, 10, 93, 58

p131 Activity 1: 160, 247, 552, 745, 999, 384, 110, 411, 200, 600, 610, 1000
Activity 2: 472, 724, 817, 217, 555, 369, 90, 195, 660, 891, 390, 990

p132 Activity 1: There are 400 units in 400. There are 40 tens in 400. There are 4 hundreds in 400.
Activity 2: Counting to 400 in **ones** takes the longest time. The quickest way to count to 400 is to count in **hundreds**.

p133
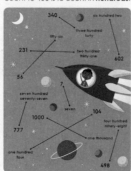

p134 Activity 1: 325, 612, 1000, 206, 840
Activity 2: five hundred twenty-four, six hundred three, seven hundred fourteen, eight hundred thirty, one thousand

p135 Activity 1: 415, 251, 769, 990, 304
Activity 2: 244 = 200 + 40 + 4;
618 = 600 + 10 + 8; 735 = 700 + 30 + 5;
470 = 400 + 70; 205 = 200 + 5

p136 253 < 300, 304 = 304, 210 > 209, 900 < 1000

p137 Activity 1: 604 > 587, 529 < 531
734 = 734, 554 > 545, 799 < 898
899 > 200, 1000 = 1000, 909 < 910
333 < 422, 654 > 456, 853 = 853
1000 > 999, 659 < 660, 100 < 1000

p138 3, 48, 177, 425, 692, 823, 989, 1000
1, 86, 231, 523, 683, 855, 923, 999
8, 28, 101, 376, 396, 723, 834, 1000
11, 42, 393, 499, 501, 835, 888, 1000
2, 82, 83, 202, 210, 733, 734, 921
0, 6, 90, 124, 462, 562, 832, 1000

p139

There are 1010 ants on the page.

Addition

p140 5 + 4 = **9**, 3 + 6 = **9**, 9 + 1 = **10**
1 + 7 = **8**, 2 + 3 = **5**, 4 + 2 = **6**
8 + 2 = **10**, 3 + 5 = **8**, 2 + 6 = **8**
4 + 3 = **7**, 5 + 2 = **7**, 7 + 2 = **9**
9 + 1 = **10**, 7 + 1 = **8**, 4 + 4 = **8**
6 + 2 = **8**, 3 + 3 = **6**, 2 + 5 = **7**
2 + 2 = **4**, 5 + 3 = **8**, 3 + 4 = **7**
7 + 3 = **10**, 5 + 5 = **10**, 1 + 8 = **9**

p141 10 toy cars, 15 ducklings, 12 neighbors, 20 shoes, 16 songs, 20 dinosaurs

p142 Activity 1: cars: even; apples: odd
Activity 2: orange numbers: 15, 33, 89, 221, 845, 999
Blue numbers: 22, 56, 100, 110, 558, 1000

p143 Activity 1: **5**; 10 = 5 + 5
7; 14 = 7 + 7
9; 18 = 9 + 9
10; 20 = 10 + 10
50; 100 = 50 + 50
Activity 2: T, F, T

p144 Activity 1: Left column: 10, 9, 8, 7, 6, 5, 4, 3, 2, 1
Right column: 10, 9, 8, 7, 6, 5, 4, 3, 2, 1
Activity 2:
⑥+④+ 7 = 10 + 7 = **17**
5 +②+⑧= 10 + 5 = **15**
①+ 4 +⑨= 10 + 4 = **14**
9 +⑤+⑤= 10 + 9 = **19**
4 +⑥+④= 10 + 4 = **14**

p145 Activity 1: 3 + 9 = 3 + 7 + 2 = 10 + 2 = **12**
6 + 8 = 6 + 4 + 4 = 10 + 4 = **14**
5 + 6 = 5 + **5** + 1 = 10 + 1 = **11**
8 + 9 = 8 + 2 + 7 = 10 + 7 = **17**
7 + 6 = 7 + **3** + 3 = 10 + 3 = **13**
Activity 2: 5 + 6 + 1 + 4 + 5 = 10 + 10 + 1 = **21**
6 + 1 + 9 + 3 + 7 = 10 + 10 + 6 = **26**
2 + 7 + 8 + 4 + 3 = 10 + 10 + 4 = **24**
3 + 5 + 5 + 0 + 7 = 10 + 10 + 0 = **20**
5 + 5 + 5 + 8 + 5 = 10 + 10 + 8 = **28**

p146 9 + 7: I take **1** from 7 and give it to the 9.
9 + 7 = 10 + 6 = **16**
9 + 5: I take **1** from 5 and give it to the 9.
9 + 5 = 10 + 4 = **14**
8 + 4: I take **2** from 4 and give it to the 8.
8 + 4 = 10 + 2 = **12**
9 + 2: I take **1** from **2** and give it to the 9.
9 + 2 = 10 + 1 = **11**
8 + 6: I take **2** from **6** and give it to the 8.
8 + 6 = 10 + **4** = **14**

p147 37 + 21 = 37 + **20** + 1 = **58**
37 →⁺¹⁰→ 47 →⁺¹⁰→ 57 →⁺¹→ 58
63 + 23 = 63 + **20** + 3 = **86**
63 →⁺¹⁰→ 73 →⁺¹⁰→ 83 →⁺¹→ →⁺¹→ 86
58 + 33 = 58 + **30** + 3 = **91**
58 →⁺¹⁰→ 68 →⁺¹⁰→ 78 →⁺¹⁰→ 88 →⁺¹→ →⁺¹→ →⁺¹→ 91
75 + 24 = 75 + **20** + 4 = **99**
75 →⁺¹⁰→ 85 →⁺¹⁰→ 95 →⁺¹→ →⁺¹→ →⁺¹→ →⁺¹→ 99

p148 4 + 20 + 4 = **28**
So, 46 + **28** = **74**
2 + 30 + 5 = **37**
So, 28 + **37** = **65**   28 →⁺²→ 30 →⁺³⁰→ 60 →⁺⁵→ 65
4 + 40 + 5 = **49**
So, 46 + **49** = **95**   46 →⁺⁴→ 50 →⁺⁴⁰→ 90 →⁺⁵→ 95
1 + 30 + 7 = **38**
So, 19 + **38** = **57**   19 →⁺¹→ 20 →⁺³⁰→ 50 →⁺⁷→ 57
5 + 20 + 4 = **29**
So, 65 + **29** = **94**   65 →⁺⁵→ 70 →⁺²⁰→ 90 →⁺⁴→ 94

p149 15 + 3 = 10 + 5 + 3 = 10 + 8 = **18**
11 + 6 = 10 + 1 + 6 = 10 + 7 = **17**
16 + 2 = 10 + 6 + 2 = 10 + 8 = **18**
24 + 4 = 20 + 4 + 4 = 20 + 8 = **28**
57 + 2 = 50 + 7 + 2 = 50 + 9 = **59**
32 + 7 = 30 + 2 + 7 = 30 + 9 = **39**
63 + 5 = 60 + 3 + 5 = 60 + 8 = **68**
91 + 8 = 90 + 1 + 8 = 90 + 9 = **99**
55 + 5 = 50 + 5 + 5 = 50 + 10 = **60**

p150 27 + 41 = (20 + 40) + (7 + 1) = 60 + 8 = **68**
65 + 34 = (60 + 30) + (5 + 4) = 90 + 9 = **99**
72 + 26 = (70 + 20) + (2 + 6) = 90 + 8 = **98**
45 + 23 = (40 + 20) + (5 + 3) = 60 + 8 = **68**
18 + 71 = (10 + 70) + (8 + 1) = 80 + 9 = **89**
56 + 43 = (50 + 40) + (6 + 3) = 90 + 9 = **99**
88 + 11 = (80 + 10) + (8 + 1) = 90 + 9 = **99**
71 + 27 = (70 + 20) + (1 + 7) = 90 + 8 = **98**
35 + 62 = (30 + 60) + (5 + 2) = 90 + 7 = **97**

p151 215 + 573 = (200 + 500) + (10 + 70) + (5 + 3) = 700 + 80 + 8 = **788**
725 + 152 = (700 + 100) + (20 + 50) + (5 + 2) = 800 + 70 + 7 = **877**
362 + 335 = (300 + 300) + (60 + 30) + (2 + 5) = 600 + 90 + 7 = **697**
624 + 241 = (600 + 200) + (20 + 40) + (4 + 1) = 800 + 60 + 5 = **865**
537 + 432 = (500 + 400) + (30 + 30) + (7 + 2) = 900 + 60 + 9 = **969**
123 + 321 = (100 + 300) + (20 + 20) + (3 + 1) = 400 + 40 + 4 = **444**
777 + 212 = (700 + 200) + (70 + 10) + (7 + 2) = 900 + 80 + 9 = **989**
544 + 242 = (500 + 200) + (40 + 40) + (4 + 2) = 700 + 80 + 6 = **786**
811 + 188 = (800 + 100) + (10 + 80) + (1 + 8) = 900 + 90 + 9 = **999**

p152 62 + 34 = 96, 47 + 21 = 68, 16 + 61 = 77
271 + 426 = 697, 342 + 350 = 692
671 + 106 = 777

p153 72 + 25 = 97, 55 + 44 = 99, 86 + 13 = 99
34 + 62 = 96, 12 + 46 = 58, 81 + 18 = 99
24 + 41 = 65
213 + 452 = 665, 625 + 374 = 999
413 + 330 = 743, 502 + 222 = 724
420 + 422 = 842, 600 + 235 = 835
713 + 804 = 1517

p154 99 + 25: I take 1 from 25 and give it to 99.
99 + 25 = 100 + **24** = **124**
98 + 42: I take **2** from 42 and give it to 98.
98 + 42 = 100 + **40** = **140**
97 + 33: I take **3** from 33 and give it to 97.
97 + 33 = 100 + **30** = **130**
199 + 23: I take **1** from 23 and give it to 199.
199 + 23 = 200 + **22** = **222**
298 + 47: I take **2** from 47 and give it to 298.
298 + 47 = 300 + **45** = **345**
397 + 54: I take **3** from 54 and give it to 397.
397 + 54 = 400 + **51** = **451**
598 + 31: I take **2** from 31 and give it to 598.
598 + 31 = 600 + **29** = **629**

p155 56 + 39 = (56 + 40) − 1 = **96** − 1 = **95**

Left column

$42 + 19 = (42 + 20) - 1 = 62 - 1 = 61$
$66 + 28 = (66 + 30) - 2 = 96 - 2 = 94$
$14 + 59 = (14 + 60) - 1 = 74 - 1 = 73$
$25 + 48 = (25 + 50) - 2 = 75 - 2 = 73$
$74 + 18 = (74 + 20) - 2 = 94 - 2 = 92$
$33 + 58 = (33 + 60) - 2 = 93 - 2 = 91$

p156 $36 + 198 = (36 + 200) - 2 = 236 - 2 = 234$
$55 + 299 = (55 + 300) - 1 = 355 - 1 = 354$
$47 + 297 = (47 + 300) - 3 = 437 - 3 = 344$
$65 + 398 = (65 + 400) - 2 = 465 - 2 = 463$
$74 + 599 = (74 + 600) - 1 = 674 - 1 = 673$
$46 + 498 = (46 + 500) - 2 = 546 - 2 = 544$
$53 + 897 = (53 + 900) - 3 = 953 - 3 = 950$

p157 $6 + 5 = 11; 30 + 20 = 50; 11 + 50 = 61$
$7 + 8 = 15; 50 + 10 = 60; 15 + 60 = 75$
$34 + 8 = 42$ ⟶ $48 + 25 = 73$
$25 + 27 = 52$ ⟶ $68 + 16 = 84$
$39 + 33 = 72$ ⟶ $57 + 34 = 91$
$53 + 48 = 101$

p158 $148 + 74 = 222$ ⟶ $273 + 49 = 322$
$192 + 129 = 321$ ⟶ $364 + 136 = 500$
$266 + 266 = 532$ ⟶ $444 + 457 = 901$
$635 + 305 = 940$ ⟶ $328 + 274 = 602$
$548 + 188 = 736$ ⟶ $720 + 280 = 1000$
$499 + 501 = 1000$

p159 20 books, 98 children learning to swim, 73 children learning judo, 68 customers, 68 passengers, 622 children saw the movie.

p160 ● ● ●
There are **2** rows. Each row has **3** dots.
There are **3** columns. Each column has **2** dots.
Altogether, there are **6** dots.

● ● ● ● ●
● ● ● ● ●
There are **2** rows. Each row has **5** dots.
There are **5** columns. Each column has **2** dots.
Altogether, there are **10** dots.

There are **4** rows. Each row has **3** dots.
There are **3** columns. Each column has **4** dots.
Altogether, there are **12** dots.

There are **3** rows. Each row has **3** dots.
There are **3** columns. Each column has **3** dots.
Altogether, there are **9** dots.
$5 + 5 + 5 = 15$
$3 + 3 + 3 + 3 + 3 = 15$
$2 + 2 + 2 + 2 = 8$
$4 + 4 = 8$

p161
$4 + 4 + 4 = 12$
$3 + 3 + 3 + 3 = 12$
$5 + 5 = 10$
$2 + 2 + 2 + 2 + 2 = 10$
$6 + 6 + 6 = 18$
$3 + 3 + 3 + 3 + 3 + 3 = 18$

Middle column

Subtraction

p162
$5 - 2 = 3$
$5 - 3 = 2$
$5 - 4 = 1$
$5 - 1 = 4$
$6 - 4 = 2$
$6 - 2 = 4$
$6 - 3 = 3$
$6 - 3 = 3$

p163
$7 - 3 = 4$
$7 - 4 = 3$
$7 - 5 = 2$
$7 - 2 = 5$
$8 - 3 = 5$
$8 - 5 = 3$
$8 - 2 = 6$
$8 - 6 = 2$

p164
$9 - 4 = 5$
$9 - 5 = 4$
$9 - 3 = 6$
$9 - 6 = 3$
$9 - 7 = 2$
$9 - 2 = 7$
$9 - 8 = 1$
$9 - 1 = 8$

–	10	9	8	7	6	5	4	3	2	1
1	9	8	7	6	5	4	3	2	1	0
2	8	7	6	5	4	3	2	1	0	
3	7	6	5	4	3	2	1	0		
4	6	5	4	3	2	1	0			
5	5	4	3	2	1	0				
6	4	3	2	1	0					
7	3	2	1	0						
8	2	1	0							
9	1	0								
10	0									

p165 $8 - 4 = 4, 3 - 1 = 2, 9 - 6 = 3$
$7 - 3 = 4, 5 - 2 = 3, 6 - 3 = 3$
$2 - 1 = 1, 10 - 7 = 3, 4 - 2 = 2$
$4 - 3 = 1, 5 - 3 = 2, 7 - 2 = 5$
$9 - 5 = 4, 7 - 5 = 2, 4 - 1 = 3$
$6 - 4 = 2, 3 - 2 = 1, 2 - 2 = 0$
$8 - 2 = 6, 9 - 7 = 2, 5 - 4 = 1$
$7 - 4 = 3, 6 - 4 = 2, 4 - 3 = 5$

p166 5 mice, 13 cupcakes, 6 comics, 9 candies, 8 cookies, 4 T-shirts

Right column

p167 Activity 1: Left column: 0, 1, 2, 3, 4, 5, 6, 7, 8, 9. Right column: 10, 9, 8, 7, 6, 5, 4, 3, 2, 1
Activity 2: $18 - 8 = $ **10**, $13 - 3 = $ **10**, $20 - 10 = $ **10**
$17 - 7 = $ **10**, $19 - 9 = $ **10**, $16 - 6 = $ **10**
$11 - 1 = $ **10**, $15 - 5 = $ **10**, $12 - 2 = $ **10**
$14 - 4 = $ **10**, $10 - 0 = $ **10**, $20 - 10 = $ **10**

p168 Activity 1: $\text{⑩} - 4 - \text{⑥} = 10 - 4 = 6$
$\text{⑮} \text{⑤} - 2 = 10 - 2 = 8$
$\text{⑲} \text{⑨} - 4 = 10 - 4 = 6$
$\text{⑰} - 6 \text{⑦} = 10 - 6 = 4$
$\text{⑭} \text{④} - 8 = 10 - 8 = 2$
Activity 2: $\text{㉒} \text{㉒} - 3 \text{②} = 20 - 3 = 17$
$\text{㉗} \text{⑦} - 5 = 20 - 5 = 15$
$\text{㉔} - 6 \text{④} = 20 - 6 = 14$
$\text{㉖} \text{⑥} - 2 = 20 - 2 = 18$
$\text{㉙} - 7 \text{⑨} = 20 - 7 = 13$

p169 $37 - 20 = $ **17**, $54 - 10 = $ **44**, $78 - 20 = $ **58**
$63 - 30 = $ **33**, $72 - 40 = $ **32**, $90 - 30 = $ **60**
$86 - 30 = $ 56, $50 - 30 = $ 20, $34 - 10 = $ 24
$62 - 20 = $ **42**, $68 - 40 = $ 28, $100 - 30 = $ 70

p170 $13 - 6 = 4 + 3 = 7$
$6 \xrightarrow{+4} 10 \xrightarrow{+3} 13$
$16 - 7 = 3 + 6 = 9$
$7 \xrightarrow{+3} 10 \xrightarrow{+6} 16$
$11 - 3 = 7 + 1 = 8$
$3 \xrightarrow{+7} 10 \xrightarrow{+1} 11$
$15 - 8 = 2 + 5 = 7$
$8 \xrightarrow{+2} 10 \xrightarrow{+5} 15$

p171 $74 - 35 = 5 + 30 + 4 = 39$
$35 \xrightarrow{+5} 40 \xrightarrow{+30} 70 \xrightarrow{+4} 74$
$41 - 27 = 3 + 10 + 1 = 14$
$27 \xrightarrow{+3} 30 \xrightarrow{+10} 40 \xrightarrow{+1} 41$
$55 - 28 = 2 + 20 + 5 = 27$
$28 \xrightarrow{+2} 30 \xrightarrow{+20} 50 \xrightarrow{+5} 55$
$82 - 46 = 4 + 30 + 2 = 36$
$46 \xrightarrow{+4} 50 \xrightarrow{+30} 80 \xrightarrow{+2} 82$

p172 $83 - 62 = (80 - 60) + (3 - 2) = 20 + 1 = 21$
$59 - 37 = (50 - 30) + (9 - 7) = 20 + 2 = 22$
$66 - 55 = (60 - 50) + (6 - 5) = 10 + 1 = 11$
$47 - 31 = (40 - 30) + (7 - 1) = 10 + 6 = 16$
$99 - 35 = (90 - 30) + (9 - 5) = 60 + 4 = 64$
$36 - 16 = (30 - 10) + (6 - 6) = 20 + 0 = 20$
$61 - 40 = (60 - 40) + (1 - 0) = 20 + 1 = 21$
$45 - 42 = (40 - 40) + (5 - 2) = 0 + 3 = 3$
$97 - 87 = (90 - 80) + (7 - 7) = 10 + 0 = 10$

p173 $76 - 52 = $ **24**, $83 - 40 = $ **43**
$638 - 425 = $ **213**, $594 - 370 = $ **224**,
$467 - 106 = $ **361**

p174 Activity 1: $96 - 35 = $ **61**, $75 - 41 = $ **34**,
$38 - 16 = $ **22**, $55 - 33 = $ **22**,
$96 - 63 = $ **33**, $61 - 40 = $ **21**,
$99 - 82 = $ **17**
Activity 2: $756 - 535 = $ **221**, $958 - 327 = $ **631**
$635 - 425 = $ **210**, $538 - 215 = $ **323**,
$945 - 830 = $ **115**, $444 - 210 = $ **234**,
$773 - 632 = $ **141**, $362 - 351 = $ 11

p175 $54 - 19 = (54 - 20) + 1 = 34 + 1 = 35$
$36 - 28 = (36 - 30) + 2 = 6 + 2 = 8$
$47 - 29 = (47 - 30) + 1 = 17 + 1 = 18$
$55 - 37 = (55 - 40) + 3 = 15 + 3 = 18$
$93 - 48 = (93 - 50) + 2 = 43 + 2 = 45$

p176 $65 - 29$: I will add **1** to both sides of the problem.
$65 - 29 = $ **66** $- $ **30** $= $ **36**
$74 - 18$: I will add **2** to both sides of the problem.
$74 - 18 = $ **76** $- $ **20** $= $ **56**
$56 - 39$: I will add **1** to both sides of the problem.
$56 - 39 = $ **57** $- $ **40** $= $ **17**
$45 - 17$: I will add **3** to both sides of the problem.
$45 - 17 = $ **48** $- $ **20** $= $ **28**

73 – 48: I will add **2** to both sides of the problem.
73 – 48 = **75 – 50 = 25**
92 – 27: I will add **3** to both sides of the problem.
92 – 27 = **95 – 30 = 65**

p177 55 – 32: I will subtract **2** from both sides of the problem.
55 – 32 = **53 – 30 = 23**
88 – 54: I will subtract **4** from both sides of the problem.
88 – 54 = **84 – 50 = 34**
56 – 33: I will subtract **3** from both sides of the problem.
56 – 33 = **53 – 30 = 23**
67 – 24: I will subtract **4** from both sides of the problem.
67 – 24 = **63 – 20 = 43**
89 – 71: I will subtract **1** from both sides of the problem.
89 – 71 = **88 – 70 = 18**
94 – 52: I will subtract **2** from both sides of the problem.
94 – 52 = **92 – 50 = 42**

p178 Activity 1: I can't take 6 from 5, so I borrow 10 from **50. 15 – 6 = 9**
The tens column subtraction is now:
40 – 20 = 20. So, 55 – 26 = **29**
I can't take 5 from 3, so I borrow 10 from **80.**
13 – 5 = 8
The tens column subtraction is now:
70 – 40 = 30. So, 83 – 45 = **38.**
Activity 2: 94 – 47 = **47,** 77 – 48 = **29**
42 – 15 = **27,** 74 – 37 = **37,** 66 – 29 = **37**

p179 534 – 247 = **287,** 647 – 429 = **218,**
777 – 488 = **289,** 475 – 387 = **88,**
925 – 336 = **589,** 463 – 273 = **190,**
614 – 325 = **289,** 548 – 255 = **293,**
724 – 456 = **268,** 548 – 479 = **69,**
884 – 326 = **558,** 273 – 77 = **196,**
371 – 274 = **97,** 956 – 766 = **190,**
184 – 96 = **88**

p180 7 children, 6 balls, 30 children, 45 children, 25 problems, 29 children

p181 5 strawberries each, 2 cookies each, 4 sandwiches each, 3 carrots each

Shapes and Measurements

p182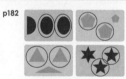

p183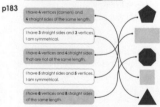

p184 Activity 2: building: vertical, pencil: horizontal, keyboard: horizontal, umbrella: vertical, ruler: horizontal, feather: vertical

p185

Activity 2: Pentagons: T, T, F, Heptagons: T, T, F, Semicircles: T, F, F

p186
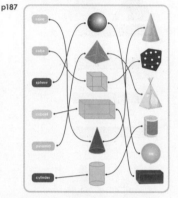
cubes – blue
cuboids – yellow
spheres – red
pyramids – green
cylinders – orange

A cube has 6 faces and 12 edges.
A cuboid has 6 faces and 12 edges.
A cylinder has 3 faces and 2 edges.
A pyramid has 5 faces and 8 edges.
A sphere has 1 face and 0 edges.

p187
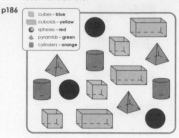
cone
cube
sphere
cuboid
pyramid
cylinder

p188 Activity 1: 35 inches, 4 years old, 15 inches
Activity 2: 5 feet, 5 feet, 3 feet, June and July

p189 5 types of fruit, 15 pineapples, 10 more plums than apples, 75 oranges and bananas, the most: oranges, the fewest: pineapples

p191 Activity 1: You need **2** halves to make a whole. You need **3** thirds to make a whole. You need **4** quarters to make a whole.
Activity 2: one part of each shape should be blue, and two parts should be red.
Activity 3: all three parts of each shape should be green.
Activity 4: ⅔, ½, ¾

p192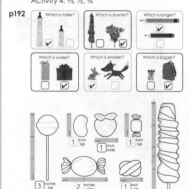
Which is taller? Which is shorter? Which is longer?
Which is wider? Which is smaller? Which is bigger?

p193 Activity 1: The table is **3** chairs long. The shelf is **7** books long. The racket is **9** balls long.
Activity 2: lizard: **12** inches, sandwich: **4** inches.

---

p194 Activity 1: Tom is **taller** than Carl. The monkey is **shorter** than the elephant.
Activity 2: 3 ft, 5 ft, 4 ft, 3 ft, 6 ft, 1 ft

p195
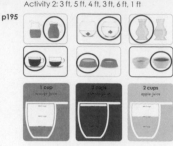
1 cup orange juice
3 cups smoothie
2 cups apple juice

Activity 3: **2** cups are in 1 pint. **2** pints are in 1 quart. **4** cups are in 1 quart.

p196 Activity 1: hotter: hot drink, colder: igloo
Activity 2: A: **20°F,** B: **90°F,** C: **40°F,** D: **80°F,** E: **10°F,** F: **60°F**
Activity 3: coldest: **E,** hottest, **B**

p197 Activity 1: heaviest: dog, luggage, chair, television
Activity 2: More than 100 lb: sofa, panda, pony, baby giraffe
Less than 100 lb: potatoes, dog, keyboard, book, straw bale, melon

p198 Activity 1: It is quarter-past eight. It is half-past ten. It is quarter to two.

two o'clock   half-past seven   quarter to ten

Activity 3: 2:00 p.m., 7:00 a.m., 11:00 p.m.

p199 Activity 1: half-past seven, quarter-past five, eleven o'clock, quarter to nine, quarter-past nine, half-past three, quarter to five.
Activity 2: 05:30, 06:15, 07:45

Social Studies

p201 Activity 2: subway: urban, tractor: rural, skyscrapers: urban, houses: suburban, cows: rural, sidewalk scene: suburban

p203 Activity 1: icebergs: polar climate, jungle: tropical climate, snow-covered house: continental climate, desert: dry climate, city: mild climate

p204 Activity 1: house, trailer, houseboat, apartment

p205 Activity 1: blue text: picture 2, green text: picture 4, pink text: picture 1, orange text: picture 3

p206 plane: airport, mountains: mountains, train: train station, building with cross: hospital, building with awning: store, river: river, building with clock: school, trees: national park

p207 Building D3 is the **hospital.** Building C2 is the **school.** Natural feature A1 is the **national park.** The **river** is in D1 and E2. The building in A4 is the **airport.**

p208 Activity 2: The store is **north** of the school. The hospital is **east** of the airport. The ranger's station is **west** of the national park. The river is **south** of the mountains.

p209 **The library** is three squares east of the park. **The airport** is two squares north of the library. **The bank** is one square south of the post office. **The museum** is three squares west of the hospital. **The post office** is two squares north and two squares east of the park. **The school** is one square north and three squares west of the store.

p210

p211 Activity 2: Pacific, Indian, Atlantic, Arctic

C	R	E	P	A	C	I	F	I	C
A	R	E	O	C	F	U	G	T	I
D	T	H	I	L	I	T	I	I	C
E	I	I	A	U	K	V	N	A	A
A	C	B	A	G	R	U	C	D	I
J	I	P	D	N	U	Z	A	I	P
A	G	W	R	A	T	R	J	A	I
G	U	V	Y	X	F	I	M	N	K
A	R	C	T	I	C	P	C	O	J
U	C	A	R	T	E	A	C	U	T

p212

The **frogs** have the largest population. The **leopards** have the smallest population. The **orangutans** and **toucans** have the same size populations.

p213 Deforestation is harmful to the environment because many animals die.
Plastic pollution is harmful to the environment because it ends up in landfill or in the oceans. Animals swallow it or become trapped in it.

p215 Malala was born in **1997**. In 2008, the Taliban rulers said **girls could not go to school**. Malala set up a charity **to help girls get an education**. Malala received the **Nobel Peace Prize** in 2014.

Science

p216

p217 You might find a fossil in **sedimentary rock**. You would find **igneous rock** near a volcano. You might find crystals in **metamorphic rock**. **Igneous rock** is sometimes filled with tiny bubbles. You might find smooth layers in **metamorphic rock**.

p218

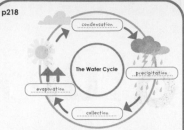

The Water Cycle — condensation, precipitation, collection, evaporation

p219

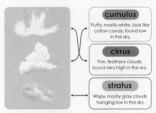

cumulus
Fluffy, mostly white, look like cotton candy, found low in the sky.

cirrus
Thin, feathery clouds, found very high in the sky.

stratus
Wispy, mostly gray clouds hanging low in the sky.

p220

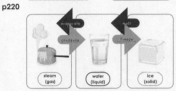

steam (gas), water (liquid), ice (solid)

p221

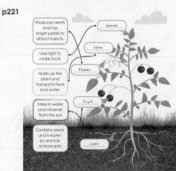

Produces seeds and has bright petals to attract insects. — leaves
Uses light to make food. — stem
Holds up the plant and transports food and water. — flower
Takes in water and minerals from the soil. — fruit
Contains seeds and is eaten by animals and people. — roots

p222

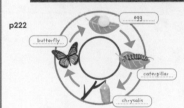

egg, butterfly, caterpillar, chrysalis

Activity 2: The butterfly life cycle has **four** stages. First, a female butterfly lays an **egg** on a leaf. A few days later, the egg **hatches** and a **caterpillar** comes out. It eats and eats, growing bigger and **bigger**. When it is fully grown, it spins a **chrysalis** around itself. After a few weeks, the chrysalis splits open and a **butterfly** comes out.

p223

antennae, head, thorax, leg, wings, abdomen

Activity 2: ladybug, wasp, dragonfly, worm

p224 Mammals, Birds, Reptiles, Amphibians, Fish

p225 A tiger is a mammal. An alligator is a reptile. A bear is a mammal. A shark is a fish. An eagle is a bird. A frog is an amphibian.

p226 1 baby, 2 toddler, 3 child, 4 teenager, 5 adult, 6 elderly person

p228

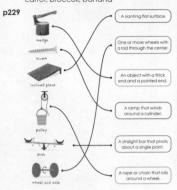

Activity 2: healthy foods: corn, apple, carrot, broccoli, banana

p229

A slanting flat surface. — wedge
One or more wheels with a rod through the center. — screw
An object with a thick end and a pointed end. — inclined plane
A ramp that winds around a cylinder. — pulley
A straight bar that pivots about a single point. — lever
A rope or chain that rolls around a wheel. — wheel and axle

p230 Images showing more friction: walking in hiking boots, rolling a car on carpet, shoes with deep tread, bathtub with a non-slip mat

p231 The ends of magnets are called **poles**. One end is the **north** pole and the other is the **south** pole. When we put opposite poles near each other, they **pull** toward each other. We say the poles attract. When we put the same poles near each other, they **push** away from each other. We say the poles **repel**.
Activity 2: the magnet will attract the scissors, screw, and key.

p232 Renewable energy sources: solar panels, water mill, windmills × 2
Nonrenewable energy sources: coal fire, wood fire, gas in truck, gas cylinder

p233 Activity 1: human, fuel, electric cables, batteries

Congratulations!

Good Work Award!

Name: ....

has successfully completed the

Grade 2

Jumbo Workbook

Date: ....

Search this page for the stickers you need.

Page 6

Page 10

Page 16

Page 18

Page 21

Reward stickers

Search this page for the stickers you need.

READING

Page **27**

Pages **28–29**

Page **30**

Page **32**

Page **34**

Pages **36–37**

Page **38**

Page **45**

Reward stickers

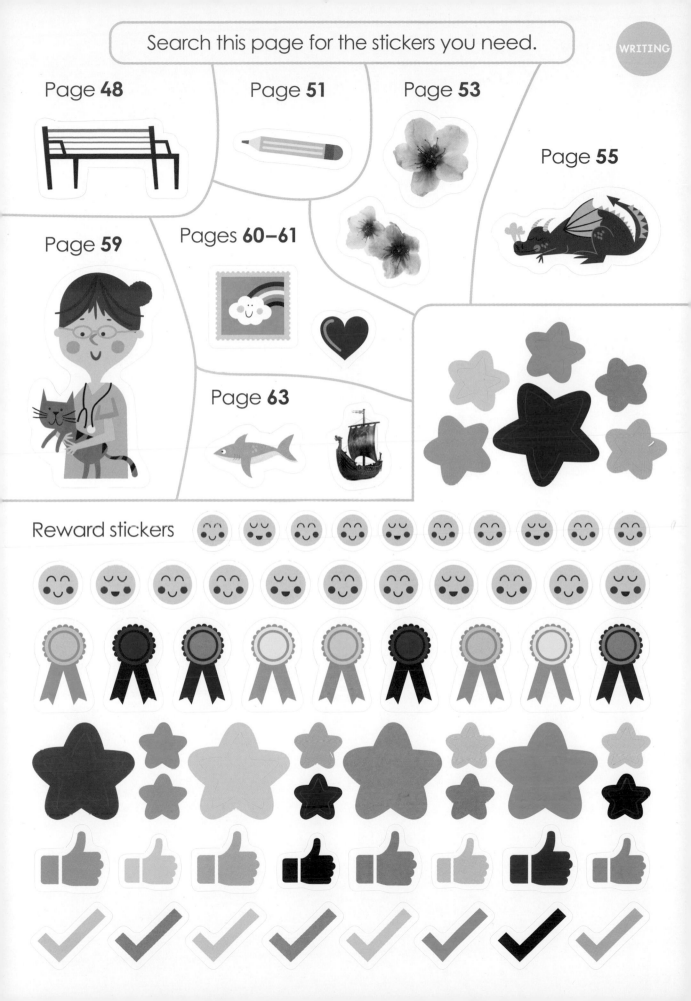

Page 66

Page 71

Page 74

Page 80

Page 81

Page 82

Reward stickers

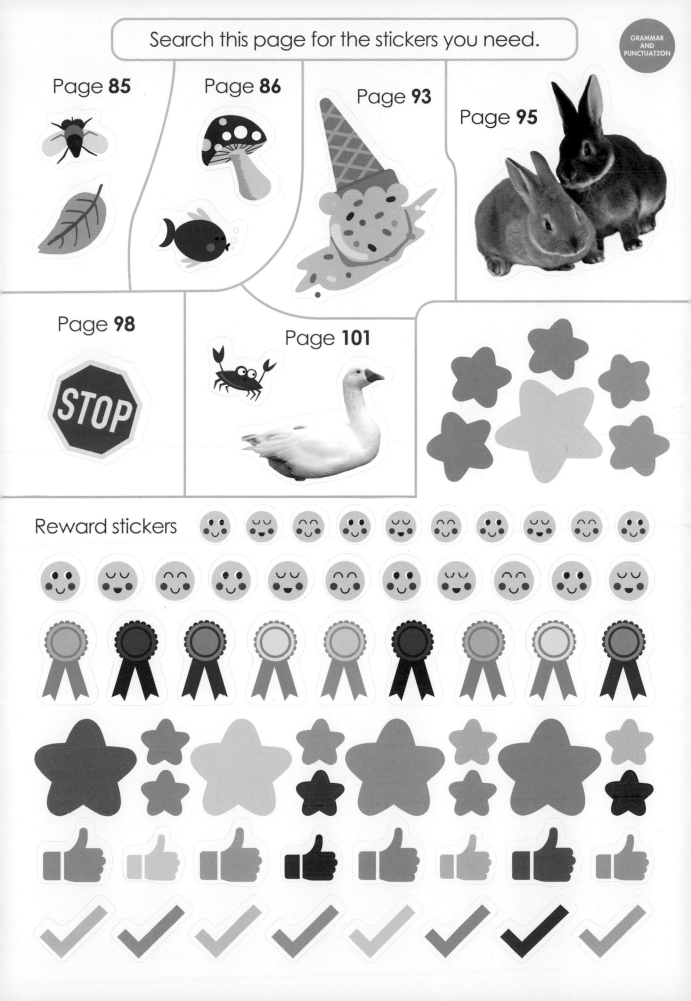

Search this page for the stickers you need.

GRAMMAR
AND
PUNCTUATION

Page **85**

Page **86**

Page **93**

Page **95**

Page **98**

STOP

Page **101**

Reward stickers

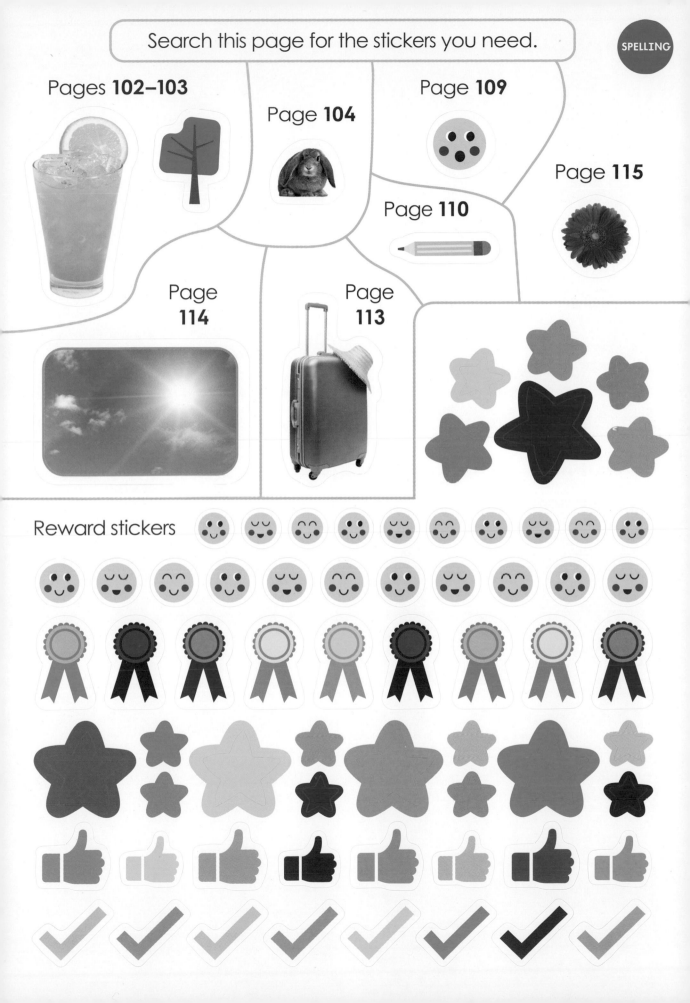

Search this page for the stickers you need.

SPELLING

Pages 102–103

Page 104

Page 109

Page 115

Page 110

Page 114

Page 113

Reward stickers

Search this page for the stickers you need.

COUNTING TO 1000

Page 123

Page 125

Page 126

Page 131

Page 133

Page 135

Page 137

Reward stickers

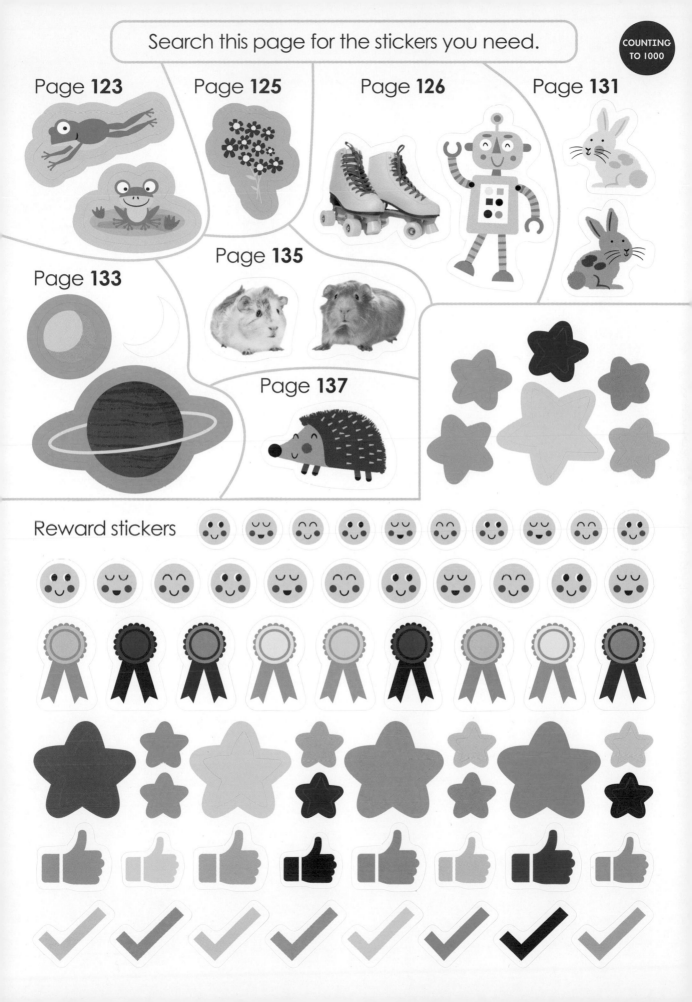

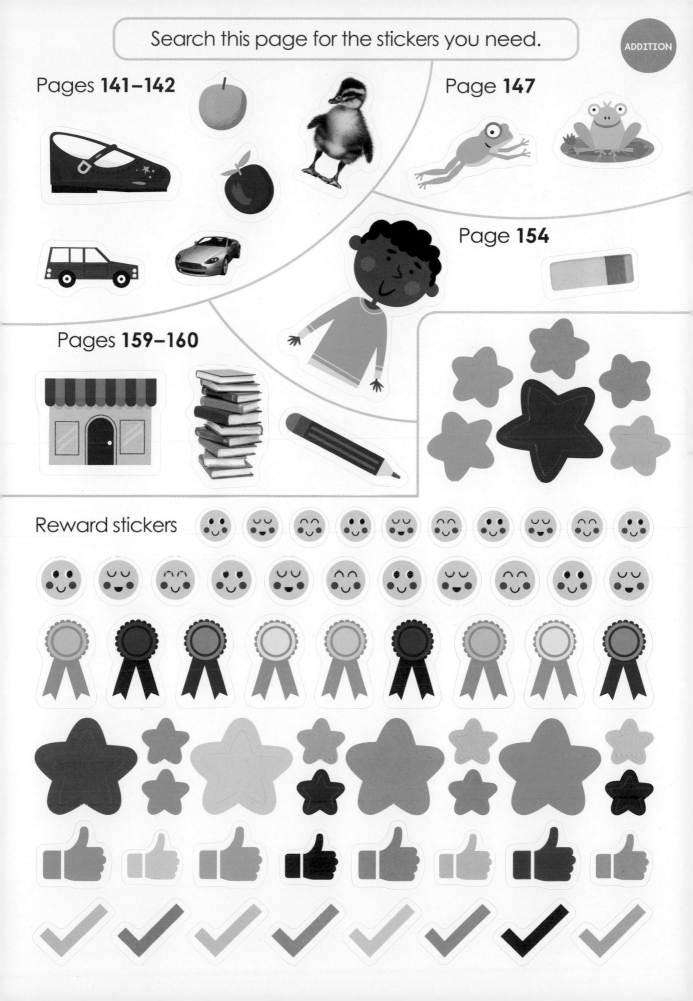

Search this page for the stickers you need.

Page 165

Page 166

Page 168

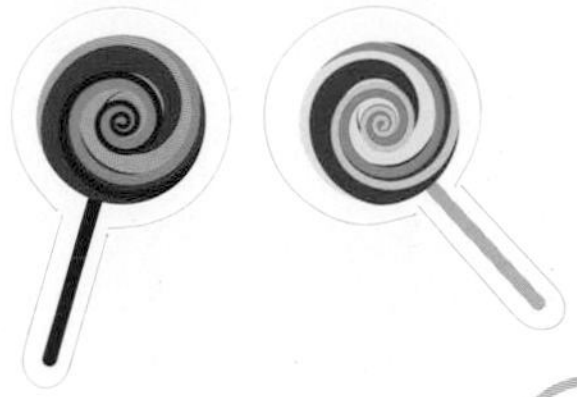

Page 173

Page 180

Reward stickers

Search this page for the stickers you need.

Page **185**

Page **194**

Page **199**

Page **196**

Reward stickers

Page **205**

Page **210**

We all live together on the world.

Page **214**

Reward stickers

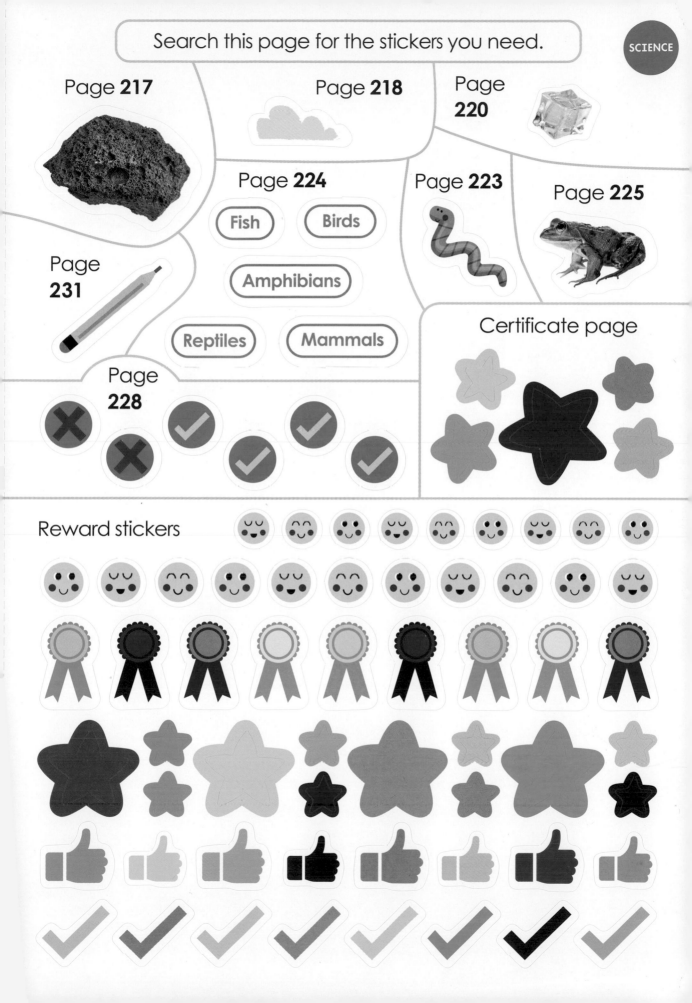

Search this page for the stickers you need.

SCIENCE

Page **217**

Page **218**

Page **220**

Page **224**

Fish   Birds

Amphibians

Reptiles   Mammals

Page **223**

Page **225**

Page **231**

Certificate page

Page **228**

Reward stickers